National Response Framework

Second Edition
May 2013

Homeland
Security

Executive Summary

The National Response Framework is a guide to how the Nation responds to all types of disasters and emergencies. It is built on scalable, flexible, and adaptable concepts identified in the National Incident Management System to align key roles and responsibilities across the Nation. This Framework describes specific authorities and best practices for managing incidents that range from the serious but purely local to large-scale terrorist attacks or catastrophic natural disasters. The National Response Framework describes the principles, roles and responsibilities, and coordinating structures for delivering the core capabilities required to respond to an incident and further describes how response efforts integrate with those of the other mission areas. **This Framework is always in effect, and elements can be implemented at any time.** The structures, roles, and responsibilities described in this Framework can be partially or fully implemented in the context of a threat or hazard, in anticipation of a significant event, or in response to an incident. Selective implementation of National Response Framework structures and procedures allows for a scaled response, delivery of the specific resources and capabilities, and a level of coordination appropriate to each incident.

The Response mission area focuses on ensuring that the Nation is able to respond effectively to all types of incidents that range from those that are adequately handled with local assets to those of catastrophic proportion that require marshaling the capabilities of the entire Nation. The objectives of the Response mission area define the capabilities necessary to save lives, protect property and the environment, meet basic human needs, stabilize the incident, restore basic services and community functionality, and establish a safe and secure environment moving toward the transition to recovery.[1] The Response mission area includes 14 core capabilities: planning, public information and warning, operational coordination, critical transportation, environmental response/health and safety, fatality management services, infrastructure systems, mass care services, mass search and rescue operations, on-scene security and protection, operational communications, public and private services and resources, public health and medical services, and situational assessment.

The priorities of response are to save lives, protect property and the environment, stabilize the incident and provide for basic human needs. The following principles establish fundamental doctrine for the Response mission area: engaged partnership, tiered response, scalable, flexible, and adaptable operational capabilities, unity of effort through unified command, and readiness to act.

Scalable, flexible, and adaptable coordinating structures are essential in aligning the key roles and responsibilities to deliver the Response mission area's core capabilities. The flexibility of such structures helps ensure that communities across the country can organize response efforts to address a variety of risks based on their unique needs, capabilities, demographics, governing structures, and non-traditional partners. This Framework is not based on a one-size-fits-all organizational construct, but instead acknowledges the concept of tiered response which emphasizes that response to incidents should be handled at the lowest jurisdictional level capable of handling the mission.

In implementing the National Response Framework to build national preparedness, partners are encouraged to develop a shared understanding of broad-level strategic implications as they make critical decisions in building future capacity and capability. The whole community should be

---

[1] As with all activities in support of the National Preparedness Goal, activities taken under the response mission must be consistent with all pertinent statutes and policies, particularly those involving privacy and civil and human rights, such as the Americans with Disabilities Act of 1990, Rehabilitation Act of 1973, and Civil Rights Act of 1964.

engaged in examining and implementing the strategy and doctrine contained in this Framework, considering both current and future requirements in the process.

Table of Contents

Introduction

The National Response Framework (NRF) is an essential component of the National Preparedness System mandated in Presidential Policy Directive (PPD) 8: National Preparedness. PPD-8 is aimed at strengthening the security and resilience of the United States through systematic preparation for the threats that pose the greatest risk to the security of the Nation. PPD-8 defines five mission areas— Prevention, Protection, Mitigation, Response, and Recovery—and mandates the development of a series of policy and planning documents to explain and guide the Nation's collective approach to ensuring and enhancing national preparedness. The NRF sets the doctrine for how the Nation builds, sustains, and delivers the response core capabilities identified in the National Preparedness Goal (the Goal). The Goal establishes the capabilities and outcomes the Nation must accomplish across all five mission areas in order to be secure and resilient.

> **Prevention:** The capabilities necessary to avoid, prevent, or stop a threatened or actual act of terrorism. As defined by PPD-8, the term "prevention" refers to preventing imminent threats.
>
> **Protection:** The capabilities necessary to secure the homeland against acts of terrorism and manmade or natural disasters.
>
> **Mitigation:** The capabilities necessary to reduce loss of life and property by lessening the impact of disasters.
>
> **Response:** The capabilities necessary to save lives, protect property and the environment, and meet basic human needs after an incident has occurred.
>
> **Recovery:** The capabilities necessary to assist communities affected by an incident to recover effectively.

Framework Purpose and Organization

The NRF is a guide to how the Nation responds to all types of disasters and emergencies. It is built on scalable, flexible, and adaptable concepts identified in the National Incident Management System (NIMS)[2] to align key roles and responsibilities across the Nation. The NRF describes specific authorities and best practices for managing incidents that range from the serious but purely local to large-scale terrorist attacks or catastrophic[3] natural disasters.

> This document supersedes the NRF that was issued in January 2008. It becomes effective 60 days after publication.

The term "response," as used in the NRF, includes actions to save lives, protect property and the environment, stabilize communities, and meet basic human needs following an incident. Response also includes the execution of emergency plans and actions to support short-term recovery. The NRF describes doctrine for managing any type of disaster or emergency regardless of scale, scope, and complexity. This Framework explains common response disciplines and processes that have been

---

[2] http://www.fema.gov/emergency/nims

[3] A catastrophic incident is defined as any natural or manmade incident, including terrorism, that results in extraordinary levels of mass casualties, damage, or disruption severely affecting the population, infrastructure, environment, economy, national morale, or government functions.

developed at all levels of government (local, state, tribal, territorial, insular area,[4] and Federal) and have matured over time.

To support the Goal, the objectives of the NRF are to:

- Describe scalable, flexible, and adaptable coordinating structures, as well as key roles and responsibilities for integrating capabilities across the whole community,[5] to support the efforts of local, state, tribal, territorial, insular area, and Federal governments in responding to actual and potential incidents

- Describe, across the whole community, the steps needed to prepare for delivering the response core capabilities

- Foster integration and coordination of activities within the Response mission area

- Outline how the Response mission area relates to the other mission areas, as well as the relationship between the Response core capabilities and the core capabilities in other mission areas

- Provide guidance through doctrine and establish the foundation for the development of the supplemental Response Federal Interagency Operational Plan (FIOP).

The NRF is composed of a base document, Emergency Support Function (ESF) Annexes, Support Annexes, and Incident Annexes (see Figure 1). The annexes provide detailed information to assist with the implementation of the NRF.

- **ESF Annexes** describe the Federal coordinating structures that group resources and capabilities into functional areas that are most frequently needed in a national response.

- **Support Annexes** describe the essential supporting processes and considerations that are most common to the majority of incidents.

- **Incident Annexes** describe the unique response aspects of incident categories.

---

[4] Per the Stafford Act, insular areas include Guam, the Commonwealth of the Northern Mariana Islands, American Samoa, and the U.S. Virgin Islands. Other statutes or departments and agencies may define the term insular area differently.

[5] Whole community includes: individuals, families, households, communities, the private and nonprofit sectors, faith-based organizations, and local, state, tribal, territorial, and Federal governments. Whole community is defined in the National Preparedness Goal as "a focus on enabling the participation in national preparedness activities of a wider range of players from the private and nonprofit sectors, including nongovernmental organizations and the general public, in conjunction with the participation of Federal, state, and local governmental partners in order to foster better coordination and working relationships." The National Preparedness Goal may be found online at http://www.fema.gov/ppd8.

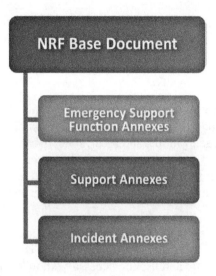

Figure 1: Organization of the NRF

Evolution of the Framework

This NRF is currently the most mature of the National Planning Frameworks because it builds on 20 years of Federal response guidance. The Federal Response Plan published in 1992 focused largely on Federal roles and responsibilities. The establishment of the Department of Homeland Security (DHS) and the emphasis on the development and implementation of common incident management and response principles led to the development of the National Response Plan (NRP) in 2004. The NRP broke new ground by integrating all levels of government, the private sector, and nongovernmental organizations (NGOs) into a common incident management framework. In 2008, the NRP was superseded by the first NRF, which streamlined the guidance and integrated lessons learned from Hurricane Katrina and other incidents.

This NRF reiterates the principles and concepts of the 2008 version of the NRF and implements the new requirements and terminology of PPD-8. By fostering a holistic approach to response, this NRF emphasizes the need for the involvement of the whole community. Along with the National Planning Frameworks for other mission areas, this document now describes the all-important integration and inter-relationships among the mission areas of Prevention, Protection, Mitigation, Response, and Recovery.

Relationship to NIMS

The response protocols and structures described in the NRF align with NIMS. NIMS provides the incident management basis for the NRF and defines standard command and management structures. Standardizing national response doctrine on NIMS provides a consistent, nationwide template to enable the whole community to work together to prevent, protect against, mitigate, respond to, and recover from the effects of incidents regardless of cause, size, location, or complexity.

All of the components of the NIMS—including preparedness, communications and information management, resource management, and command and management—support response. The NIMS concepts of multi-agency coordination and unified command are described in the command and management component of NIMS. These two concepts are essential to effective response operations because they address the importance of: (1) developing a single set of objectives; (2) using a collective, strategic approach; (3) improving information flow and coordination; (4) creating a common understanding of joint priorities and limitations; (5) ensuring that no agency's legal authorities are compromised or neglected; and (6) optimizing the combined efforts of all participants under a single plan.

Intended Audience

The NRF is intended to be used by the whole community. This all-inclusive concept focuses efforts and enables a full range of stakeholders—individuals, families, communities, the private and nonprofit sectors, faith-based organizations, and local, state, tribal, territorial, insular area, and Federal governments—to participate in national preparedness activities and to be full partners in incident response. Government resources alone cannot meet all the needs of those affected by major disasters. All elements of the community must be activated, engaged, and integrated to respond to a major or catastrophic incident.

Engaging the whole community is essential to the Nation's success in achieving resilience and national preparedness. Individual and community preparedness is a key component to this objective. By providing equal access to acquire and use the necessary knowledge and skills, the whole community contributes to and benefits from national preparedness. This includes children; individuals with disabilities and others with access and functional needs;[6] those from religious, racial and ethnically diverse backgrounds; and people with limited English proficiency. Their contributions must be integrated into preparedness efforts, and their needs must be incorporated into planning for and delivering the response core capabilities as defined in the Goal.[7]

Although the NRF is intended to provide guidance for the whole community, it focuses especially on the needs of those who are involved in delivering and applying the response core capabilities defined in the National Preparedness Goal. This includes emergency management practitioners, community leaders, and government officials who must collectively understand and assess the needs of their respective communities and organizations and determine the best ways to organize and strengthen their resiliency.

Scope

The NRF describes structures for implementing nationwide response policy and operational coordination for all types of domestic incidents.[8] This section describes the scope of the Response mission area, the guiding principles of response doctrine and their application, and how risk informs response planning.

The Response mission area focuses on ensuring that the Nation is able to respond effectively to all types of incidents that range from those that are adequately handled with local assets to those of catastrophic proportion that require marshaling the capabilities of the entire Nation. The objectives of the Response mission area define the capabilities necessary to save lives, protect property and the

---

[6] Access and functional needs includes ensuring the equal access and meaningful participation of all individuals, without discrimination.

[7] For further information, see the Core Capabilities section.

[8] A domestic incident may have international and diplomatic impacts and implications that call for coordination and consultations with foreign governments and international organizations. The NRF also applies to the domestic response to incidents of foreign origin that impact the United States. See the International Coordination Support Annex for more information.

environment, meet basic human needs, stabilize the incident, restore basic services and community functionality, and establish a safe and secure environment moving toward the transition to recovery.[9]

The NRF describes the principles, roles and responsibilities, and coordinating structures for delivering the core capabilities required to respond to an incident and further describes how response efforts integrate with those of the other mission areas. **The NRF is always in effect, and elements can be implemented at any time.** The structures, roles, and responsibilities described in the NRF can be partially or fully implemented in the context of a threat or hazard, in anticipation of a significant event, or in response to an incident. Selective implementation of NRF structures and procedures allows for a scaled response, delivery of the specific resources and capabilities, and a level of coordination appropriate to each incident.

In this Framework, the term incident includes actual or potential emergencies and disasters resulting from all types of threats and hazards, ranging from accidents and natural disasters to cyber intrusions and terrorist attacks. The NRF's structures and procedures address incidents where Federal support to local, state, tribal, territorial, and insular area governments is coordinated under the Robert T. Stafford Disaster Relief and Emergency Assistance Act (Stafford Act), as well as incidents where Federal departments and agencies exercise other authorities and responsibilities.

Nothing in the NRF is intended to alter or impede the ability of any local, state, tribal, territorial, insular area, or Federal government department or agency to carry out its authorities or meet its responsibilities under applicable laws, executive orders, and directives.

Guiding Principles

The priorities of response are to save lives, protect property and the environment, stabilize the incident and provide for basic human needs. The following principles establish fundamental doctrine for the Response mission area: (1) engaged partnership, (2) tiered response, (3) scalable, flexible, and adaptable operational capabilities, (4) unity of effort through unified command, and (5) readiness to act. These principles are rooted in the Federal system and the Constitution's division of responsibilities between state and Federal governments. These principles reflect the history of emergency management and the distilled wisdom of responders and leaders across the whole community.

Engaged Partnership

Effective partnership relies on engaging all elements of the whole community, as well as international partners in some cases. This also includes survivors who may require assistance and who may also be resources to support community response and recovery.

Those who lead emergency response efforts must communicate and support engagement with the whole community by developing shared goals and aligning capabilities to reduce the risk of any jurisdiction being overwhelmed in times of crisis. Layered, mutually supporting capabilities of individuals, communities, the private sector, NGOs, and governments at all levels allow for coordinated planning in times of calm and effective response in times of crisis. Engaged partnership

---

[9] As with all activities in support of the National Preparedness Goal, activities taken under the response mission must be consistent with all pertinent statutes and policies, particularly those involving privacy and civil and human rights, such as the Americans with Disabilities Act of 1990, Rehabilitation Act of 1973, and Civil Rights Act of 1964.

and coalition building includes ongoing clear, consistent, effective,[10] and culturally appropriate communication and shared situational awareness about an incident to ensure an appropriate response.

Tiered Response

Most incidents begin and end locally and are managed at the local level. These incidents typically require a unified response from local agencies, the private sector, and NGOs. Some may require additional support from neighboring jurisdictions or state governments. A smaller number of incidents require Federal support or are led by the Federal Government.[11] National response protocols are structured to provide tiered levels of support when additional resources or capabilities are needed.

Scalable, Flexible, and Adaptable Operational Capabilities

As incidents change in size, scope, and complexity, response efforts must adapt to meet evolving requirements. The number, type, and sources of resources must be able to expand rapidly to meet the changing needs associated with a given incident and its cascading effects. As needs grow and change, response processes must remain nimble and adaptable. The structures and processes described in the NRF must be able to surge resources from the whole community. As incidents stabilize, response efforts must be flexible to support the transition from response to recovery.

Unity of Effort through Unified Command

Effective, unified command is indispensable to response activities and requires a clear understanding of the roles and responsibilities of all participating organizations.[12] The Incident Command System (ICS), a component of NIMS, is an important element in ensuring interoperability across multi-jurisdictional or multi-agency incident management activities. Unified command, a central tenet of ICS, enables organizations with jurisdictional authority or functional responsibility for an incident to support each other through the use of mutually developed incident objectives. Each participating agency maintains its own authority, responsibility, and accountability.

Readiness to Act

Effective response requires a readiness to act that is balanced with an understanding of the risks and hazards responders face. From individuals, families, and communities to local, state, tribal, territorial, insular area, and Federal governments, national response depends on the ability to act decisively. A forward-leaning posture is imperative for incidents that may expand rapidly in size, scope, or complexity, as well as incidents that occur without warning. Decisive action is often required to save lives and protect property and the environment. Although some risk to responders may be

---

[10] Information, warnings, and communications associated with emergency management must ensure effective communication, such as through the use of appropriate auxiliary aids and services (e.g., interpreters, captioning, alternate format documents), for individuals with disabilities and provide meaningful access to limited English proficient individuals.

[11] Certain incidents such as a pandemic or cyber event may not be limited to a specific geographic area and may be managed at the local, state, tribal, territorial, insular area, or Federal level depending on the nature of the incident.

[12] The Incident Command System's "unified command" concept is distinct from the military use of this term. Concepts of "command" and "unity of command" have distinct legal and cultural meanings for military forces and military operations. Military forces always remain under the control of the military chain of command and are subject to redirection or recall at any time. Military forces do not operate under the command of the incident commander or under the unified command structure, but they do coordinate with response partners and work toward a unity of effort while maintaining their internal chain of command.

unavoidable, all response personnel are responsible for anticipating and managing risk through proper planning, organizing, equipping, training, and exercising. Effective response relies on disciplined processes, procedures, and systems to communicate timely, accurate, and accessible information about an incident's cause, size, and current status to the public, responders, and other stakeholders.

Risk Basis

The NRF leverages the findings from the Strategic National Risk Assessment (SNRA) to build and deliver the response core capabilities. The SNRA identifies the threats and hazards that pose the greatest risk to the Nation. These findings affirm the need for an all-hazards, capability-based approach to preparedness to ensure that all types of scenarios are accounted for. The risks and threats identified by SNRA include the following:

- Natural hazards—including hurricanes, earthquakes, wildfires, and floods—present a significant and varied risk across the country.

- A virulent strain of pandemic influenza could kill hundreds of thousands of Americans, affect millions more, and result in considerable economic loss. Additional human and animal infectious diseases, including those previously undiscovered, may also present significant risks.

- Technological and accidental hazards, such as dam failures or chemical substance spills or releases, have the potential to cause extensive fatalities and severe economic impacts, and the likelihood of occurrence may increase due to aging infrastructure.

- Terrorist organizations or affiliates may seek to acquire, build, and use weapons of mass destruction. Conventional terrorist attacks, including those by lone actors employing explosives and armed attacks, present a continued risk to the Nation.

- Cyber attacks can have catastrophic consequences and may also have cascading effects such as power grid or financial system failures.

No single threat or hazard exists in isolation. As an example, a hurricane can lead to flooding, dam failures, and hazardous materials spills. The Goal, therefore, focuses on core capabilities that can be applied to deal with cascading effects. Since many incidents occur with little or no warning, these capabilities must be able to be delivered in a no-notice environment.

In order to establish the basis for these capabilities, planning factors drawn from a number of different scenarios are used to develop the Response FIOP, which supplements the NRF. Refer to the Operational Planning section for additional details on planning assumptions.

Roles and Responsibilities

Effective response depends on integration of the whole community and all partners executing their roles and responsibilities. This section describes those roles and responsibilities and sharpens the focus on identifying who is involved with the Response mission area. It also addresses what the various partners must do to deliver the response core capabilities and to integrate successfully with the Prevention, Protection, Mitigation, and Recovery mission areas.

An effective, unified national response requires layered, mutually supporting capabilities. Individuals and families, communities, the private sector, NGOs, and local, state, tribal, territorial, insular area, and Federal governments should each understand their respective roles and responsibilities and how to complement each other in achieving shared goals. All elements of the whole community play prominent roles in developing the core capabilities needed to respond to incidents. This includes developing plans, conducting assessments and exercises, providing and directing resources and capabilities, and gathering lessons learned. These activities require that all partners understand how they fit within and are supported by the structures described in the NRF.

Emergency management staff in all jurisdictions have a fundamental responsibility to consider the needs of all members of the whole community, including children; individuals with disabilities and others with access and functional needs; those from religious, racial, and ethnically diverse backgrounds; and people with limited English proficiency. The potential contributions of all these individuals toward delivering core capabilities during incident response (e.g., through associations and alliances that serve these populations) should be incorporated into planning efforts.

Staff must also consider those who own or have responsibility for animals both as members of the community who may be affected by incidents and as a potential means of supporting response efforts. This includes those with household pets, service and assistance animals, working dogs, and livestock, as well as those who have responsibility for wildlife, exotic animals, zoo animals, research animals, and animals housed in shelters, rescue organizations, breeding facilities, and sanctuaries.

Individuals, Families, and Households

Although not formally part of emergency management operations, individuals, families, and households play an important role in emergency preparedness and response. By reducing hazards in and around their homes by efforts such as raising utilities above flood level or securing unanchored objects against the threat of high winds, individuals reduce potential emergency response requirements. Individuals, families, and households should also prepare emergency supply kits and emergency plans so they can take care of themselves and their neighbors until assistance arrives. Information on emergency preparedness can be found at many community, state, and Federal emergency management Web sites, such as http://www.ready.gov.

Individuals can also contribute to the preparedness and resilience of their households and communities by volunteering with emergency organizations (e.g., the local chapter of the American Red Cross, Medical Reserve Corps, or Community Emergency Response Teams [CERTs]) and completing emergency response training courses. Individuals, families, and households should make preparations with family members who have access and functional needs or medical needs. Their plans should also include provisions for their animals, including household pets or service animals. During an actual disaster, emergency, or threat, individuals, households, and families should monitor emergency communications and follow guidance and instructions provided by local authorities.

Communities

Communities are groups that share goals, values, and institutions. They are not always bound by geographic boundaries or political divisions. Instead, they may be faith-based organizations, neighborhood partnerships, advocacy groups, academia, social and community groups, and associations. Communities bring people together in different ways for different reasons, but each provides opportunities for sharing information and promoting collective action. Engaging these groups in preparedness efforts, particularly at the local and state levels, is important to identifying their needs and taking advantage of their potential contributions.

Nongovernmental Organizations

NGOs play vital roles at the local, state, tribal, territorial, insular area government, and national levels in delivering important services, including those associated with the response core capabilities. NGOs include voluntary, racial and ethnic, faith-based, veteran-based, and nonprofit organizations that provide sheltering, emergency food supplies, and other essential support services. NGOs are inherently independent and committed to specific interests and values. These interests and values drive the groups' operational priorities and shape the resources they provide. NGOs bolster government efforts at all levels and often provide specialized services to the whole community, as well as to certain members of the population including children; individuals with disabilities and others with access and functional needs; those from religious, racial, and ethnically diverse backgrounds; and people with limited English proficiency. NGOs are key partners in preparedness activities and response operations.

Examples of NGO contributions include:

- Training and managing volunteer resources

- Identifying physically accessible shelter locations and needed supplies to support those displaced by an incident

- Providing emergency commodities and services, such as water, food, shelter, assistance with family reunification, clothing, and supplies for post-emergency cleanup

- Supporting the evacuation, rescue, care, and sheltering of animals displaced by the incident

- Providing search and rescue, transportation, and logistics services and support

- Identifying those whose needs have not been met and helping to provide assistance

- Providing health, medical, mental health, and behavioral health resources

- Assisting, coordinating, and providing disability-related assistance and functional needs support services (FNSS)

- Providing language assistance services to individuals with limited English proficiency.

At the same time that NGOs support response core capabilities, they may also require government assistance. When planning for local community emergency management resources, government organizations should consider the potential need to better enable NGOs to perform their essential response functions.

Some NGOs are officially designated as support elements to national response capabilities:

- **The American Red Cross.** The American Red Cross is chartered by Congress to provide relief to survivors of disasters and help people prevent, prepare for, and respond to emergencies. The Red Cross has a legal status of "a federal instrumentality" and maintains a special relationship with the Federal Government. In this capacity, the American Red Cross supports several ESFs and the delivery of multiple core capabilities.

- **National Voluntary Organizations Active in Disaster (VOAD).**[13] National VOAD is the forum where organizations share knowledge and resources throughout the disaster cycle— preparation, response, and recovery—to help disaster survivors and their communities. National VOAD is a consortium of approximately 50 national organizations and 55 territorial and state equivalents.

- **Volunteers and Donations.** Incident response operations frequently exceed the resources of government organizations. Volunteers and donors support response efforts in many ways, and governments at all levels must plan ahead to incorporate volunteers and donated resources into

---

[13] Additional information is available at http://www.nvoad.org.

response activities. The goal of volunteer and donations management is to support jurisdictions affected by disasters through close collaboration with the voluntary organizations and agencies. The objective is to manage the influx of volunteers and donations to voluntary agencies and all levels of government before, during, and after an incident. Additional information may be found in the Volunteers and Donations Management Support Annex.

Private Sector Entities

Private sector organizations contribute to response efforts through partnerships with each level of government. They play key roles before, during, and after incidents. Private sector entities include large, medium, and small businesses; commerce, private cultural and educational institutions; and industry, as well as public/private partnerships that have been established specifically for emergency management purposes. Private sector organizations may play any of the roles described in Table 1 and may play multiple roles simultaneously. During an incident, key private sector partners should have a direct link to emergency managers and, in some cases, be involved in the decision making process. Strong integration into response efforts can offer many benefits to both the public and private sectors.

Table 1: Private Sector Roles

Category	Role in This Category
Affected Organization/Component of the Nation's Economy	Private sector organizations may be affected by direct or indirect consequences of an incident. Such organizations include entities that are significant to local, regional, and national economic recovery from an incident. Examples include major employers and suppliers of key commodities or services. As key elements of the national economy, it is important for private sector organizations of all types and sizes to take every precaution necessary to boost resilience, the better to stay in business or resume normal operations quickly.
Affected Infrastructure	Critical infrastructure—such as privately owned transportation and transit, telecommunications, utilities, financial institutions, hospitals, and other health regulated facilities—should have effective business continuity plans.[14]
Regulated and/or Responsible Party	Owners/operators of certain regulated facilities or hazardous operations may be legally responsible for preparing for and preventing incidents and responding when an incident occurs. For example, Federal regulations require owners/operators of nuclear power plants to maintain emergency plans and to perform assessments, notifications, and training for incident response.
Response Resource	Private sector entities provide response resources (donated or compensated) during an incident—including specialized teams, essential services, equipment, and advanced technologies—through local public-private emergency plans or mutual aid and assistance agreements or in response to requests from government and nongovernmental-volunteer initiatives.

---

[14] Additional information on the protection of critical infrastructure can be found in the National Protection Framework, the National Infrastructure Protection Plan, and the NRF Critical Infrastructure Support Annex.

Category	Role in This Category
Partner With Federal/State/Local Emergency Organizations	Private sector entities may serve as partners in state and local emergency preparedness and response organizations and activities and with Federal sector-specific agencies.
Components of the Nation's Economy	As key elements of the national economy, private sector resilience and continuity of operations planning, as well as recovery and restoration from incidents, represent essential homeland security activities.

A fundamental responsibility of private sector organizations is to provide for the welfare of their employees in the workplace. In addition, some businesses play an essential role in protecting critical infrastructure systems and implementing plans for the rapid reestablishment of normal commercial activities and critical infrastructure operations following a disruption. In many cases, private sector organizations have immediate access to commodities and services that can support incident response, making them key potential contributors of resources necessary to deliver the core capabilities. How the private sector participates in response activities varies based on the type of organization and the nature of the incident.

Examples of key private sector activities include:

- Addressing the response needs of employees, infrastructure, and facilities

- Protecting information and maintaining the continuity of business operations

- Planning for, responding to, and recovering from incidents that impact their own infrastructure and facilities

- Collaborating with emergency management personnel to determine what assistance may be required and how they can provide needed support

- Contributing to communication and information sharing efforts during incidents

- Planning, training, and exercising their response capabilities

- Providing assistance specified under mutual aid and assistance agreements

- Contributing resources, personnel, and expertise; helping to shape objectives; and receiving information about the status of the community.

Local Governments

The responsibility for responding to natural and manmade incidents that have recognizable geographic boundaries generally begins at the local level with individuals and public officials in the county, parish, city, or town affected by an incident. The following paragraphs describe the responsibilities of specific local officials who have emergency management responsibilities.

Chief Elected or Appointed Official

Jurisdictional chief executives are responsible for the public safety and welfare of the people of their jurisdiction. These officials provide strategic guidance and resources across all five mission areas. Chief elected or appointed officials must have a clear understanding of their emergency management roles and responsibilities and how to apply the response core capabilities as they may need to make decisions regarding resources and operations during an incident. Lives may depend on their decisions. Elected and appointed officials also routinely shape or modify laws, policies, and budgets to aid preparedness efforts and improve emergency management and response capabilities. The local chief executive's response duties may include:

- Obtaining assistance from other governmental agencies

- Providing direction for response activities

- Ensuring appropriate information is provided to the public.

Emergency Manager

The jurisdiction's emergency manager oversees the day-to-day emergency management programs and activities. The emergency manager works with chief elected and appointed officials to establish unified objectives regarding the jurisdiction's emergency plans and activities. This role entails coordinating and integrating all elements of the community. The emergency manager coordinates the local emergency management program. This includes assessing the capacity and readiness to deliver the capabilities most likely required during an incident and identifying and correcting any shortfalls. The local emergency manager's duties often include:

- Advising elected and appointed officials during a response

- Conducting response operations in accordance with the NIMS

- Coordinating the functions of local agencies

- Coordinating the development of plans and working cooperatively with other local agencies, community organizations, private sector entities, and NGOs

- Developing and maintaining mutual aid and assistance agreements

- Coordinating resource requests during an incident through the management of an emergency operations center

- Coordinating damage assessments during an incident

- Advising and informing local officials and the public about emergency management activities during an incident

- Developing and executing accessible public awareness and education programs

- Conducting exercises to test plans and systems and obtain lessons learned

- Coordinating integration of the rights of individuals with disabilities, individuals from racially and ethnically diverse backgrounds, and others with access and functional needs into emergency planning and response.

Department and Agency Heads

Department and agency heads collaborate with the emergency manager during the development of local emergency plans and provide key response resources. Participation in the planning process helps to ensure that specific capabilities are integrated into a workable plan to safeguard the community. These department and agency heads and their staffs develop, plan, and train on internal policies and procedures to meet response needs safely. They also participate in interagency training and exercises to develop and maintain necessary capabilities.

State, Tribal, Territorial, and Insular Area Governments

State, tribal, territorial, and insular area governments are responsible for the health and welfare of their residents, communities, lands, and cultural heritage.

States

State governments[15] supplement local efforts before, during, and after incidents by applying in-state resources first. If a state anticipates that its resources may be exceeded, the governor[16] may request assistance from other states or the Federal Government.

Federal assistance may be available to the states under the Stafford Act and other Federal authorities. Under some Federal laws, Federal response actions may be taken without a request from the state. For example, when notified of an oil discharge or chemical release, the Environmental Protection Agency (EPA) and U.S. Coast Guard (USCG) are required to evaluate the need for Federal response and may take action without waiting for a request from state or local officials. Federal financial assistance may also be available to supplement non-Stafford Act incidents and for disability-related access and functional needs equipment. The following paragraphs describe some of the relevant roles and responsibilities of key officials.

Governor

The public safety and welfare of a state's residents are the fundamental responsibilities of every governor. The governor coordinates state resources and provides the strategic guidance for response to all types of incidents. This includes supporting local governments as needed and coordinating assistance with other states and the Federal Government. A governor also:

- In accordance with state law, may make, amend, or suspend certain orders or regulations associated with response

- Communicates to the public, in an accessible manner (e.g., effective communications to address all members of the whole community), and helps people, businesses, and organizations cope with the consequences of any type of incident

- Coordinates with tribal governments within the state

- Commands the state military forces (National Guard personnel not in Federal service and state militias)

- Coordinates assistance from other states through interstate mutual aid and assistance agreements, such as the Emergency Management Assistance Compact (EMAC)[17]

- Requests Federal assistance including, if appropriate, a Stafford Act declaration of an emergency or major disaster.

---

[15] States are sovereign entities, and the governor has responsibility for public safety and welfare. Although U.S. territories, possessions, freely associated states, and tribal governments also have sovereign rights, there are unique factors involved in working with these entities. Stafford Act assistance is available to states and to the District of Columbia, Puerto Rico, the Virgin Islands, Guam, American Samoa, and the Commonwealth of the Northern Mariana Islands, which are included in the definition of "state" in the Stafford Act. Federal disaster preparedness, response, and recovery assistance is available to the Federated States of Micronesia and the Republic of the Marshall Islands pursuant to Compacts of Free Association. The extent to which Federal response or assistance is provided to insular areas, territories, and tribes under other Federal laws is defined in those laws and supporting regulations.

[16] "Governor" is used throughout this document to refer to the chief executive of states, territories, and insular areas.

[17] A reference paper on EMAC is available at http://www.emacweb.org.

State Homeland Security Advisor

Many states have designated homeland security advisors who serve as counsel to the governor on homeland security issues and may serve as a liaison between the governor's office, the state homeland security structure, and other organizations both inside and outside of the state. The advisor often chairs a committee composed of representatives of relevant state agencies, including public safety, the National Guard, emergency management, public health, environment, agriculture, and others charged with developing prevention, protection, mitigation, response, and recovery strategies.

State Emergency Management Agency Director

All states have laws mandating the establishment of a state emergency management agency, as well as the emergency plans coordinated by that agency. The director of the state emergency management agency is responsible for ensuring that the state is prepared to deal with large-scale emergencies and coordinating the statewide response to any such incident. This includes supporting local and tribal governments as needed, coordinating assistance with other states and the Federal Government, and, in some cases, with NGOs and private sector organizations. The state emergency management agency may dispatch personnel to assist in the response and recovery effort.

National Guard

The National Guard is an important state and Federal resource available for planning, preparing, and responding to natural or manmade incidents. National Guard members have expertise in critical areas, such as emergency medical response; communications; logistics; search and rescue; civil engineering; chemical, biological, radiological, and nuclear response and planning; and decontamination.[18]

The governor may activate elements of the National Guard to support state domestic civil support functions and activities. The state adjutant general may assign members of the Guard to assist with state, regional, and Federal civil support plans.

Other State Departments and Agencies

State department and agency heads and their staffs develop, plan, and train on internal policies and procedures to meet response and recovery needs. They also participate in interagency training and exercises to develop and maintain the necessary capabilities. They are vital to the state's overall emergency management program, as they bring expertise spanning various response functions and serve as core members of the state emergency operations center (EOC) and incident command posts (ICP). Many of them have direct experience in providing accessible and vital services to the whole community during response operations. State departments and agencies typically work in close coordination with their Federal counterpart agencies during joint state and Federal responses, and under some Federal laws, they may request assistance from these Federal partners.

---

[18] The President may call National Guard forces into Federal service for domestic duties under Title 10 (e.g., in cases of invasion by a foreign nation, rebellion against the authority of the United States, or where the President is unable to execute the laws of the United States with regular forces under 10 U.S. Code §12406). When National Guardsmen are employed under Title 10 of the U.S. Code, these forces are no longer under the command of the governor. Instead, the Department of Defense assumes full command and control of National Guard forces called into Federal service.

Tribes

The United States has a trust relationship with federally-recognized Indian tribes and recognizes their right to self-government. Tribal governments are responsible for coordinating resources to address actual or potential incidents. When tribal response resources are inadequate, tribal leaders may seek assistance from states or the Federal Government. For certain types of Federal assistance, tribal governments work with the state in which they are located. For other types of Federal assistance, as sovereign entities, tribal governments can elect to work directly with the Federal Government.

Tribes are encouraged to build relationships with local jurisdictions and their states as they may have resources most readily available. The NRF's Tribal Coordination Support Annex outlines processes and mechanisms that tribal governments may use to request direct Federal assistance during an incident regardless of whether or not the incident involves a Stafford Act declaration.

Territories/Insular Areas

Territorial and insular area governments are responsible for coordinating resources to address actual or potential incidents. Due to their remote locations, territories and insular area governments often face unique challenges in receiving assistance from outside the jurisdiction quickly and often request assistance from neighboring islands, other nearby countries, states, the private sector or NGO resources, or the Federal Government. Federal assistance is delivered in accordance with pertinent Federal authorities (e.g., the Stafford Act or through other authorities of Federal departments or agencies).

Tribal/Territorial/Insular Area Leader

The tribal/territorial/insular area government leader is responsible for the public safety and welfare of the people of his/her jurisdiction. As authorized by the tribal, territorial, or insular area government, the leader:

- Coordinates resources needed to respond to incidents of all types

- In accordance with the law, may make, amend, or suspend certain orders or regulations associated with the response

- Communicates with the public in an accessible manner and helps people, businesses, and organizations cope with the consequences of any type of incident

- Commands the territory's military forces

- Negotiates mutual aid and assistance agreements with other tribes, territories, insular area governments, states, or local jurisdictions

- Can request Federal assistance under the Stafford Act.

Federal Government

The President leads the Federal Government response effort to ensure that the necessary resources are applied quickly and efficiently to large-scale and catastrophic incidents. The Federal Government maintains a wide range of capabilities and resources that may be required to deal with domestic incidents in a way that ensures the protection of privacy, civil rights, and civil liberties. To be successful, any approach to the delivery of Response capabilities will require an all-of-nation approach. All Federal departments and agencies must cooperate with one another, and with local, state, tribal, territorial, and insular area governments, community members, and the private sector to the maximum extent possible. Although Federal disaster assistance is often considered synonymous with Presidential declarations under the Stafford Act, Federal assistance can actually be provided to state and local jurisdictions, as well as to other Federal departments and agencies, through a number of different mechanisms and authorities.

For incidents in which Federal assistance is provided under the Stafford Act, the Federal Emergency Management Agency (FEMA) coordinates the assistance. For non-Stafford Act incidents, Federal response or assistance may be led or coordinated by various Federal departments and agencies consistent with their authorities.

For incidents on Federal property (e.g., National Parks, military bases) or where the Federal Government has primary jurisdiction, Federal departments or agencies may be the first responders and coordinators of Federal, state, and local activities.

Coordination of Federal Response and Assistance

The President leads the Federal Government response effort to ensure that the necessary resources are applied quickly and efficiently to large-scale and catastrophic incidents. When coordination of Federal response activities is required, it is implemented through the Secretary of Homeland Security, pursuant to Presidential directive.[19] Other Federal departments and agencies carry out their response authorities and responsibilities within this overarching construct.

Secretary of Homeland Security

Pursuant to Presidential directive, the Secretary of Homeland Security is the principal Federal official for domestic incident management. The Secretary coordinates preparedness activities within the United States to respond to and recover from terrorist attacks, major disasters, and other emergencies. As part of these responsibilities, the Secretary coordinates with Federal entities to provide for Federal unity of effort for domestic incident management. The Secretary's responsibilities also include management of the broad "emergency management" and "response" authorities of FEMA and other DHS components.

As part of these responsibilities, the Secretary of Homeland Security also provides the Executive Branch with an overall architecture for domestic incident management and coordinates the Federal response, as required. The Secretary of Homeland Security may monitor activities and activate specific response mechanisms to support other Federal departments and agencies without assuming the overall coordination of the Federal response during incidents that do not require the Secretary to coordinate the response or do not result in a Stafford Act declaration.

Unity of effort differs from unity of command. Various Federal departments and agencies may have statutory responsibilities and lead roles based upon the unique circumstances of the incident. Unity of effort provides coordination through cooperation and common interests and does not interfere with Federal departments' and agencies' supervisory, command, or statutory authorities. The Secretary ensures that overall Federal actions are unified, complete, and synchronized to prevent unfilled gaps or seams in the Federal Government's overarching effort. This coordinated approach ensures that the Federal actions undertaken by DHS and other departments and agencies are harmonized and mutually supportive. The Secretary executes these coordination responsibilities, in part, by engaging directly with the President and relevant Cabinet, department, agency, and DHS component heads as is necessary to ensure a focused, efficient, and unified Federal preparedness posture. All Federal

---

[19] Except for those activities that may interfere with the authority of the Attorney General or the FBI Director, as described in PPD-8.

departments and agencies, in turn, cooperate with the Secretary in executing domestic incident management duties.

DHS component heads may have lead response roles or other significant roles depending on the type and severity of the incident. For example, the U.S. Secret Service is the lead agency for security design, planning, and implementation of National Special Security Events (NSSEs) while the Assistant Secretary for Cybersecurity and Communications coordinates the response to significant cyber incidents.

Other Federal departments and agencies may have a lead or support role in operations coordination. When the Secretary of Homeland Security is not exercising delegated response coordination responsibilities, other Federal departments and agencies may coordinate Federal operations under their own statutory authorities, or as designated by the President, and may activate response structures applicable to those authorities. The head of the department or agency may also request the Secretary to activate other NRF structures and elements to provide additional assistance, while still retaining leadership for the response. For all incidents, Federal department and agency heads serve as advisors to the Executive Branch for their areas of responsibility. Nothing in the NRF precludes any Federal department or agency from executing their authorities.

Several Federal departments and agencies have authorities to respond to and declare specific types of disasters or emergencies apart from the Stafford Act. These authorities may be exercised independently of, concurrently with, or become part of a Federal response coordinated by the Secretary of Homeland Security, pursuant to Presidential directive. Federal departments and agencies carry out their response authorities and responsibilities within the NRF's overarching construct or under supplementary or complementary operational plans. Table 2 provides examples of scenarios in which specific Federal departments and agencies have the responsibility for coordinating response activities. This is not an all-inclusive list. Refer to the NRF Incident Annexes for more details.

Table 2: Examples of Other Federal Department and Agency Authorities

Scenario	Department/Agency	Authorities
Agricultural and Food Incident	Department of Agriculture (USDA)	The Secretary of Agriculture has the authority to declare an **extraordinary emergency** and take action due to the presence of a pest or disease of livestock that threatens livestock in the United States. (7 U.S. Code § 8306 [2007]). The Secretary of Agriculture also has the authority to declare an **extraordinary emergency** and take action due to the presence of a plant pest or noxious weed whose presence threatens plants or plant products of the United States. (7 U.S. Code § 7715 [2007]).
Public Health Emergency[20]	Department of Health and Human Services	The Secretary of the Department of Health and Human Services has the authority to take actions to protect the public health and welfare, declare a **public health emergency** and to prepare for and respond to public health emergencies. (Public Health Service Act, 42 U.S. Code §§ 201 *et seq.*).

---

[20] A declaration of a public health emergency may make available any funds appropriated to the Public Health Emergency Fund.

Scenario	Department/Agency	Authorities
Oil and Hazardous Materials Spills	EPA or USCG	The EPA and USCG have the authority to take actions to respond to oil discharges and releases of hazardous substances, pollutants, and contaminants, including leading the response. (42 U.S. Code § 9601, et seq., 33 U.S. Code § 1251 et seq.) The EPA Administrator and Commandant of the USCG[21] may also classify an oil discharge as a **Spill of National Significance** and designate senior officials to participate in the response. (40 CFR § 300.323).[22]

NOTE: These authorities may be exercised independently of, concurrently with, or become part of a Federal response coordinated by the Secretary of Homeland Security pursuant to Presidential directive.

When a Federal department, agency, or component of DHS has responsibility for directing or managing a major aspect of a response coordinated by the Secretary of Homeland Security, that organization is part of the national leadership for the incident and is represented in field, regional, and headquarters unified command and coordination organizations.

FEMA Administrator

The Administrator is the principal advisor to the President, the Secretary of Homeland Security, and the Homeland Security Council regarding emergency management. The FEMA Administrator's duties include assisting the President, through the Secretary, in carrying out the Stafford Act, operation of the National Response Coordination Center (NRCC), the effective support of all ESFs, and more generally, preparation for, protection against, response to, and recovery from all-hazards incidents. Reporting to the Secretary of Homeland Security, the FEMA Administrator is also responsible for managing the core DHS grant programs supporting homeland security activities.[23]

Attorney General

Like other Executive Branch departments and agencies, the Department of Justice and the Federal Bureau of Investigation (FBI) will endeavor to coordinate their activities with other members of the law enforcement community, and with members of the Intelligence Community, to achieve maximum cooperation consistent with the law and operational necessity.

The Attorney General has lead responsibility for criminal investigations of terrorist acts or terrorist threats, where such acts are within the Federal criminal jurisdiction of the United States. Generally acting through the FBI Director, the Attorney General, in cooperation with Federal departments and agencies engaged in activities to protect our national security, shall also coordinate the activities of the other members of the law enforcement community to detect, prevent, preempt, and disrupt terrorist attacks against the United States.

In addition, the Attorney General approves requests submitted by state governors pursuant to the Emergency Federal Law Enforcement Assistance Act for personnel and other Federal law enforcement support during incidents. The Attorney General also enforces Federal civil rights laws,

---

[21] The Commandant of the USCG coordinates the designation of a Spill of National Significance with the Secretary of Homeland Security, as appropriate.

[22] See the ESF #10 – Oil and Hazardous Materials Response Annex for more information on these authorities.

[23] See the Post-Katrina Emergency Management Reform Act, enacted as part of the FY 2007 DHS Appropriations Act, P.L. 109-295.

such as the Americans with Disabilities Act of 1990 and the Civil Rights Act of 1964. Further information on the Attorney General's role is provided in the National Prevention Framework and Prevention FIOP.

Secretary of Defense

Because of the Department of Defense's (DOD's) critical role in national defense, its resources are committed only after approval by the Secretary of Defense or at the direction of the President. Many DOD officials are authorized to respond to save lives, protect property, and mitigate human suffering under imminently serious conditions, as well as to provide support under their separate established authorities, as appropriate.[24] When DOD resources are authorized to support civil authorities, command of those forces remains with the Secretary of Defense. DOD elements in the incident area of operations and the National Guard forces under the command of a governor coordinate closely with response organizations at all levels.

Secretary of State

A domestic incident may have international and diplomatic implications that call for coordination and consultation with foreign governments and international organizations. The Secretary of State is responsible for all communication and coordination between the U.S. Government and other nations regarding the response to a domestic crisis. The Department of State also coordinates international offers of assistance and formally accepts or declines these offers on behalf of the U.S. Government based on needs conveyed by Federal departments and agencies as stated in the International Coordination Support Annex. Some types of international assistance are pre-identified, and bilateral agreements are already established. For example, the USDA/Forest Service and Department of the Interior have joint bilateral agreements with several countries for wildland firefighting support.

Director of National Intelligence

The Director of National Intelligence serves as the head of the Intelligence Community, acts as the principal advisor to the President for intelligence matters relating to national security, and oversees and directs implementation of the National Intelligence Program. The Intelligence Community, comprising 17 elements across the Federal Government, functions consistent with law, Executive Order, regulations, and policy to support the national security-related missions of the U.S. Government. It provides a range of analytic products, including those that assess threats to the homeland and inform planning, capability development, and operational activities of homeland security enterprise partners and stakeholders. In addition to intelligence community elements with specific homeland security missions, The Office of the Director of National Intelligence maintains a number of mission and support centers that provide unique capabilities for homeland security partners.

---

[24] In response to a request for assistance from a civilian authority, under imminently serious conditions, and if time does not permit approval from higher authority, DOD officials may provide an immediate response by temporarily employing the resources under their control, subject to any supplemental direction provided by higher headquarters, to save lives, prevent human suffering, or mitigate great property damage within the United States. Immediate response authority does not permit actions that would subject civilians to the use of military power that is regulatory, prescriptive, proscriptive, or compulsory. (DOD Directive 3025.18)

Other Federal Department and Agency Heads

Various Federal departments or agencies play primary, coordinating, or support roles in delivering response core capabilities. They may also have responsibilities and authorities to respond independent of any Stafford Act declaration as indicated above. Additional information regarding Federal department and agency roles in delivering core capabilities may be found in the Coordinating Structures and Integration section and in the various annexes to this Framework.

Core Capabilities

Once an incident occurs, efforts focus on saving lives, protecting property and the environment, and preserving the social, economic, cultural, and political structure of the jurisdiction. Depending on the size, scope, and magnitude of an incident, local, state, tribal, territorial, and insular area governments, and, in some cases, the Federal Government, may be called to action. The response core capabilities are a list of the activities that generally must be accomplished in incident response regardless of which levels of government are involved.

This list was developed based on the results of the SNRA which identified a variety of threats and hazards that would likely stress the Nation's response capabilities. Planners for each mission area— Prevention, Protection, Mitigation, Response, and Recovery—identified functions that would be required to deal with these threats and hazards, and these are the core capabilities. The core capabilities are distinct critical elements necessary to achieve the Goal. They provide a common vocabulary describing the significant functions that must be developed and executed across the whole community to ensure national preparedness.

This section addresses the core capabilities for the Response mission area and the actions required to build and deliver these capabilities.

Context of the Response Mission Area

By engaging the whole community to build and deliver the response core capabilities, the Nation is better prepared to respond to any threat or hazard, assist in restoring basic services and community functionality, and support the transition to recovery. The Response mission area includes 14 core capabilities—11 that apply to response and three that are common to all five mission areas. The Goal assigned specific objectives and performance thresholds for each capability from which metrics will ultimately be identified to track the Nation's progress toward achieving these objectives. Table 3 provides a summary of each response core capability and the critical tasks to achieve its objective.

Table 3: Overview of Response Core Capabilities in the National Preparedness Goal

Core Capabilities and Critical Tasks	
1. Planning *(Cross-cutting with all mission areas)*	**Objective:** Conduct a systematic process engaging the whole community, as appropriate, in the development of executable strategic, operational, and/or community-based approaches to meet defined objectives.
Critical Tasks: ■ Develop operational plans at the Federal level and in the states and territories that adequately identify critical objectives based on the planning requirements, provide a complete and integrated picture of the sequence and scope of the tasks to achieve the objectives, and are implementable within the time frame contemplated in the plan using available resources.	

Core Capabilities and Critical Tasks

2. Public Information and Warning *(Cross-cutting with all mission areas)*	**Objective:** Deliver coordinated, prompt, reliable, and actionable information to the whole community through the use of clear, consistent, accessible, and culturally and linguistically appropriate methods to effectively relay information regarding any threat or hazard and, as appropriate, the actions being taken and the assistance being made available.

Critical Tasks:
- Inform all affected segments of society by all means necessary, including accessible tools, of critical lifesaving and life-sustaining information to expedite the delivery of emergency services and aid the public in taking protective actions.
- Deliver credible messages to inform ongoing emergency services and the public about protective measures and other life-sustaining actions and facilitate the transition to recovery.

3. Operational Coordination *(Cross-cutting with all mission areas)*	**Objective:** Establish and maintain a unified and coordinated operational structure and process that appropriately integrates all critical stakeholders and supports the execution of core capabilities.

Critical Tasks:
- Mobilize all critical resources and establish command, control, and coordination structures within the affected community and other coordinating bodies in surrounding communities and across the Nation and maintain, as needed, throughout the duration of an incident.
- Enhance and maintain NIMS-compliant command, control, and coordination structures to meet basic human needs, stabilize the incident, and transition to recovery.

4. Critical Transportation	**Objective:** Provide transportation (including infrastructure access and accessible transportation services) for response priority objectives, including the evacuation of people and animals, and the delivery of vital response personnel, equipment, and services to the affected areas.

Critical Tasks:
- Establish physical access through appropriate transportation corridors and deliver required resources to save lives and to meet the needs of disaster survivors.
- Ensure basic human needs are met, stabilize the incident, transition into recovery for an affected area, and restore basic services and community functionality.

5. Environmental Response/Health and Safety	**Objective:** Ensure the availability of guidance and resources to address all hazards, including hazardous materials, acts of terrorism, and natural disasters, in support of the responder operations and the affected communities.

Critical Tasks:
- Conduct health and safety hazard assessments and disseminate guidance and resources, to include deploying hazardous materials teams, to support environmental health and safety actions for response personnel and the affected population.
- Assess, monitor, perform cleanup actions, and provide resources to meet resource requirements and to transition from sustained response to short-term recovery.

Core Capabilities and Critical Tasks	
6. Fatality Management Services	**Objective:** Provide fatality management services, including body recovery and victim identification, working with state and local authorities to provide temporary mortuary solutions, sharing information with Mass Care Services for the purpose of reunifying family members and caregivers with missing persons/remains, and providing counseling to the bereaved.
Critical Tasks: ▪ Establish and maintain operations to recover a significant number of fatalities over a geographically dispersed area.	
7. Infrastructure Systems *(Cross-cutting with Recovery mission area)*	**Objective:** Stabilize critical infrastructure functions, minimize health and safety threats, and efficiently restore and revitalize systems and services to support a viable, resilient community.
Critical Tasks: ▪ Decrease and stabilize immediate infrastructure threats to the affected population, to include survivors in the heavily-damaged zone, nearby communities that may be affected by cascading effects, and mass care support facilities and evacuation processing centers with a focus on life-sustainment and congregate care services. ▪ Re-establish critical infrastructure within the affected areas to support ongoing emergency response operations, life sustainment, community functionality, and a transition to recovery.	
8. Mass Care Services	**Objective:** Provide life-sustaining services to the affected population with a focus on hydration, feeding, and sheltering to those with the most need, as well as support for reunifying families.
Critical Tasks: ▪ Move and deliver resources and capabilities to meet the needs of disaster survivors, including individuals with access and functional needs. ▪ Establish, staff, and equip emergency shelters and other temporary housing options ensuring that shelters and temporary housing units are physically accessible for individuals with disabilities and others with access and functional needs. ▪ Move from congregate care to non-congregate care alternatives, and provide relocation assistance or interim housing solutions for families unable to return to their pre-disaster homes.	
9. Mass Search and Rescue Operations	**Objective:** Deliver traditional and atypical search and rescue capabilities, including personnel, services, animals, and assets to survivors in need, with the goal of saving the greatest number of endangered lives in the shortest time possible.
Critical Tasks: ▪ Conduct search and rescue operations to locate and rescue persons in distress, based on the requirements of state and local authorities. ▪ Initiate community-based search and rescue support operations across a wide geographically dispersed area. ▪ Ensure the synchronized deployment of local, regional, national, and international teams to reinforce ongoing search and rescue efforts and transition to recovery.	

Core Capabilities and Critical Tasks	
10. On-scene Security and Protection	**Objective:** Ensure a safe and secure environment through law enforcement and related security and protection operations for people and communities located within affected areas and for all traditional and atypical response personnel engaged in lifesaving and life-sustaining operations.

Critical Tasks:
- Establish a safe and secure environment in an affected area.
- Provide and maintain on-scene security and meet the protection needs of the affected population over a geographically dispersed area while eliminating or mitigating the risk of further damage to persons, property, and the environment.

11. Operational Communications	**Objective:** Ensure the capacity for timely communications in support of security, situational awareness, and operations by any and all means available between affected communities in the impact area and all response forces.

Critical Tasks:
- Ensure the capacity to communicate with both the emergency response community and the affected populations and establish interoperable voice and data communications between local, state, tribal, territorial, and Federal first responders.
- Re-establish sufficient communications infrastructure within the affected areas to support ongoing life-sustaining activities, provide basic human needs, and transition to recovery.

12. Public and Private Services and Resources	**Objective:** Provide essential public and private services and resources to the affected population and surrounding communities, to include emergency power to critical facilities, fuel support for emergency responders, and access to community staples (e.g., grocery stores, pharmacies, and banks) and fire and other first response services.

Critical Tasks:
- Mobilize and deliver governmental, nongovernmental, and private sector resources within and outside of the affected area to save lives, sustain lives, meet basic human needs, stabilize the incident, and transition to recovery, to include moving and delivering resources and services to meet the needs of disaster survivors.
- Enhance public and private resource and services support for an affected area.

13. Public Health and Medical Services	**Objective:** Provide lifesaving medical treatment via emergency medical services and related operations, and avoid additional disease and injury by providing targeted public health and medical support and products to all people in need within the affected area.

Critical Tasks:
- Deliver medical countermeasures to exposed populations.
- Complete triage and the initial stabilization of casualties and begin definitive care for those likely to survive their injuries.
- Return medical surge resources to pre-incident levels, complete health assessments, and identify recovery processes.

Core Capabilities and Critical Tasks	
14. Situational Assessment	**Objective:** Provide all decision makers with decision-relevant information regarding the nature and extent of the hazard, any cascading effects, and the status of the response.

Critical Tasks:

- Deliver information sufficient to inform decision making regarding immediate lifesaving and life-sustaining activities, and engage governmental, private, and civic sector resources within and outside of the affected area to meet basic human needs and stabilize the incident.
- Deliver enhanced information to reinforce ongoing lifesaving and life-sustaining activities, and engage governmental, private, and civic sector resources within and outside of the affected area to meet basic human needs, stabilize the incident, and transition to recovery.

No core capability is the responsibility of any one party or single level of government. Each requires an approach that integrates the abilities of elements in the whole community from the individual through the Federal Government, including traditional and non-traditional partners. The Nation must be prepared to deal not only with the normal type of incidents that communities handle every day, but also with incidents of catastrophic proportions. Most of the resources and functions required at the local level to deliver a given core capability are provided by local government agencies with additional members of the community assisting as needed. Catastrophic incidents require many more response assets and engagement with a broader set of partners.[25] Community involvement is vital to providing additional response support. Local residents may well be the primary source of additional manpower in the first hours and days after a catastrophic incident.

Cross-cutting Response Core Capabilities

Three response core capabilities—Planning, Public Information and Warning, and Operational Coordination—span all five mission areas. These common core capabilities are essential to the success of the other core capabilities. They help establish unity of effort among all those involved in the Response mission area.

- **Planning.** Planning makes it possible to manage the life cycle of a potential crisis, determine capability requirements, and help stakeholders learn their roles. It includes the collection, analysis, and dissemination of risk assessment data and the development of plans, procedures, mutual aid and assistance agreements, strategies, and other arrangements to perform specific missions and tasks. Governments at all levels have a responsibility to develop all-hazards response plans prior to and during an incident. Including a broad range of partners in the planning process helps ensure that the needs and potential contributions of all elements are integrated into workable plans.

- **Public Information and Warning.** For an effective response, jurisdictions must provide accurate and accessible information to decision makers and the public. This includes development of accessible message content, such as incident facts, health risk warnings, pre-incident recommendations, evacuation guidance, and other protective measures. It also includes developing strategies for when, where, how, and by whom information will be delivered and

---

[25] Given the scope and magnitude of a catastrophic incident, waivers, exceptions, and exemptions to policy, regulations, and laws may be available in order to save and sustain life, and to protect property and the environment. However, any such waivers, exceptions, and exemptions must be consistent with laws that preserve human and civil rights and protect individuals with disabilities and others with access and functional needs.

ensuring that all levels of government agree on unified messages. Information must be shared with the public and other members of the response community efficiently, effectively, and in an accessible manner. Effective public information and warning is particularly important in dealing with incidents that start small but may evolve to have greater consequences.

- **Operational Coordination.** For incident response, coordination of operations must occur both among those tasked to deliver the various response core capabilities and with those delivering the core capabilities of other mission areas. This coordination occurs through response structures based on clearly established roles, responsibilities, and reporting protocols. Using NIMS principles, structures, and coordinating processes enhances the efficiency and effectiveness of response. Specific actions to achieve this core capability may include coordinating initial actions, managing ESFs, coordinating requests for additional support, and identifying and integrating resources and capabilities.

Integration among Response Core Capabilities and Mission Areas

Interdependencies exist among many of the core capabilities. For example, organizations involved in providing Mass Care Services often rely on resources and functions from organizations that provide Critical Transportation or Public and Private Services and Resources for commodities distribution; Public Information and Warning for messaging, translators, and interpreters; and Operational Communications for reporting and communication that allows shelters to stay in touch with operations centers.

The core capabilities in various mission areas may also be linked through shared assets and services. For example, the functionality provided by geographic information systems can be applied across multiple response core capabilities, as well as core capabilities in the other four mission areas. Thus synergy among mission area resources and processes is important to maximize capabilities and minimize risk. The overarching nature of functions described in these capabilities frequently involves either support to or cooperation of several incident management partners to ensure the seamless integration and transitions among prevention, protection, mitigation, response, and recovery activities.

Potential points of intersection between the Response mission area and other mission areas include the following:

- **Prevention.** Many of the assets that are used on a day-to-day basis to perform intelligence, law enforcement, homeland security, and homeland defense can be applied to support delivery of response core capabilities such as On-Scene Security and Protection and Public Information and Warning.

- **Protection.** Protection of critical infrastructure systems and implementation of plans for the rapid restoration of commercial activities and critical infrastructure operations are crucial aspects of the Protection mission area. Many of the 18 critical infrastructure sectors[26] within the Protection mission area are also represented in the Response mission area. For example, the Public and Private Services and Resources capability depends on private sector owners and operators of critical infrastructure for achieving the capability's objective.

- **Mitigation.** Achieving the mitigation core capability preliminary targets allows for the incorporation of lessons learned in the analysis and planning processes and makes the response core capabilities more resilient and effective.

---

[26] The critical infrastructure sectors are described in the National Infrastructure Protection Plan.

- **Recovery.** Even while response activities are underway, recovery operations must begin. The emphasis on response gradually gives way to recovery operations; however, recovery core capabilities may involve some of the same functions as response core capabilities. This includes providing essential public health and safety services, restoring interrupted utility and other essential services, reestablishing transportation routes, providing food and shelter for those displaced by an incident, protecting natural and cultural resources and performing environmental compliance, ensuring equal access, reunifying children who have been displaced from their families/guardians, and reopening schools and child care centers.

These overlapping areas are identified through comprehensive planning with the whole community to ensure that they are properly addressed during response to an incident. Ensuring that IOPs properly account for the integration and transition between mission areas is essential.

Response Actions to Deliver Core Capabilities

This section describes the key tasks each major element of the whole community must accomplish to be prepared to deliver the core capabilities. More detailed concepts of operations for the delivery of the core capabilities are provided in the Response FIOP and operational plans developed by various jurisdictions, the private sector, and NGOs.

Individuals and Households

Many individuals have talents and experience that can be tapped to support core capabilities. Individuals can contribute to the delivery of response core capabilities through community organizations, by participating in community preparedness activities, such as CERT, and by ensuring that they have household/family emergency plans.[27]

Private Sector

Roles and responsibilities of private sector entities are described in the Roles and Responsibilities section. Private sector entities can assist in delivering the response core capabilities by collaborating with emergency management personnel before an incident occurs to determine what assistance may be necessary and how they can support local emergency management during response operations.[28]

Nongovernmental Organizations

NGOs manage volunteers and resources that bolster government efforts to ensure a successful incident response. Collaboration with responders, governments at all levels, and other agencies and organizations helps NGOs to tailor and direct their efforts that are necessary to accomplish and deliver the response core capabilities.

State, Tribal, and Local Actions

Communities apply NIMS principles to integrate response plans and resources across jurisdictions and departments as well as with the private sector and NGOs. Neighboring communities play a key role by providing support through a network of mutual aid and assistance agreements that identify the resources that communities may be able to share during an incident.

---

[27] Individual and household preparedness information can be located at http://www.ready.gov/make-a-plan.

[28] Additional information sharing and collaborative opportunities can be located at FEMA Private Sector Focus http://www.fema.gov/privatesector/index.shtm.

The state is the gateway to many government resources that help communities respond. When an incident grows or has the potential to grow beyond the capability of a local jurisdiction and responders cannot meet the needs with mutual aid and assistance resources, local officials contact the state. Upon receiving a request for assistance from a local or tribal government, state officials may:

- Coordinate warnings and public information through the activation of the state's public communications strategy

- Distribute supplies stockpiled to meet the needs of the emergency

- Provide technical assistance and support to meet the response and recovery needs

- Suspend or waive statutes, rules, ordinances, and orders, to the extent permitted by law, to ensure timely performance of response functions

- Implement state volunteer and donations management plans, and coordinate with the private sector and NGOs

- Order or recommend evacuations ensuring the integration and inclusion of the requirements of populations such as: children, individuals with disabilities and others with access and functional needs, those from religious, racial, and ethnically diverse communities, people with limited English proficiency, and owners of animals including household pets and service animals

- Mobilize resources to meet the requirements of individuals with disabilities and others with access and functional needs in compliance with Federal civil rights laws.

If local resources are inadequate, local authorities may seek assistance from the county emergency manager or the state. Under some Federal authorities, local jurisdictions may also seek assistance directly from the Federal Government for non-Stafford Act incidents.

State-to-State Assistance

If additional resources are required, states request assistance from other states through interstate mutual aid and assistance agreements such as EMAC. Administered by the National Emergency Management Association, EMAC is an interstate mutual aid agreement that streamlines the interstate mutual aid and assistance process.

Federal Actions

In certain circumstances, Federal departments and agencies may provide assistance or even lead response efforts consistent with their own authorities.

Federal Response and Assistance under the Stafford Act

When an incident is anticipated to exceed state resources or when the Federal Government has unique capabilities needed by states, the governor may request Federal assistance. In such cases, the affected local jurisdiction and the state, tribal, territorial, insular area, and Federal governments coordinate to provide the necessary assistance. The Federal Government may provide assistance in the form of funding, resources, and services. Federal departments and agencies respect the sovereignty and responsibilities of local, state, tribal, territorial, and insular area governments while rendering assistance that supports the affected local or state governments.

Robert T. Stafford Disaster Relief and Emergency Assistance Act

Local, state, tribal, territorial, and insular area governments do not require Federal assistance to respond to most incidents; however, when an incident is of such severity and magnitude that effective response is beyond the capabilities of the state and local governments, the governor can request Federal assistance under the Stafford Act. In certain circumstances, the President may declare an emergency without a request from a governor when the primary responsibility for response rests with the United States because the emergency involves a subject area for which, under the Constitution or laws of the United States, the United States exercises exclusive or preeminent responsibility and authority.

The Stafford Act authorizes the President to provide financial and other assistance to local, state, tribal, territorial, and insular area governments, certain private nonprofit organizations, and individuals to support response, recovery, and mitigation efforts following a Stafford Act Emergency or Major Disaster Declaration.[29] Most forms of Stafford Act assistance require a state cost share. While Federal assistance under the Stafford Act may only be delivered after a declaration, FEMA may pre-deploy Federal assets when a declaration is likely and imminent. The Stafford Act provides for two types of declarations:

- An **Emergency Declaration** is more limited in scope than a Major Disaster Declaration, provides fewer Federal programs, and is not normally associated with recovery programs. However, the President may issue an Emergency Declaration prior to an actual incident to lessen or avert the threat of a catastrophe. Generally, Federal assistance and funding are provided to meet specific emergency needs or to help prevent a catastrophe from occurring.

- A **Major Disaster Declaration** provides more Federal programs for response and recovery than an Emergency Declaration. Unlike an Emergency Declaration, a Major Disaster Declaration may only be issued after an incident.

Requesting a Stafford Act Declaration

Before requesting a declaration under the Stafford Act, the situation or disaster must be of such severity and magnitude that an effective response is beyond the capabilities of the state and the affected local governments and requires Federal assistance. The governor must take appropriate response action under state law and direct execution of the state's emergency plan. Ordinarily, the governor must ensure certain state and local actions have been taken or initiated, including:

- Surveying the affected areas to determine the extent of private and public damage

- Conducting joint preliminary damage assessments with FEMA officials to estimate the types and extent of Federal disaster assistance required

- Agreeing to provide, without cost to the Federal Government, easements and rights-of-way necessary to accomplish the work and to indemnify the Federal Government against any claims arising from such work when requesting direct Federal assistance

- Agreeing to pay the state's cost share.

The state's request for a Stafford Act declaration, addressed to the President, is submitted through the FEMA Regional Administrator, who evaluates the request and makes a recommendation to the FEMA Administrator. The FEMA Administrator, in coordination with the Secretary of Homeland Security, then makes a recommendation to the President. The governor is notified when the President has acted on the state's request and the appropriate members of Congress and Federal departments and agencies are also notified.

---

[29] The President has delegated most of his authority under the Stafford Act to the Secretary of Homeland Security, who has, in turn, delegated those authorities to the FEMA Administrator.

U.S. territories may use the same incident management and response structures and mechanisms as state governments for requesting and receiving Federal assistance. U.S. territories often pose special response challenges. Working in partnership with territorial governments, the processes and structures described in the NRF can be adapted to meet these geographic challenges through preparedness plans and the pre-staging of assets.

Territorial governments may receive federally coordinated response for U.S. possessions, including insular area governments. The freely associated states of the Federated States of Micronesia and the Republic of the Marshall Islands[30] may also receive assistance. Stafford Act assistance is available to Puerto Rico, the U.S. Virgin Islands, Guam, American Samoa, and the Commonwealth of the Northern Mariana Islands, which are included in the definition of "state" in the Stafford Act.

Proactive Response to Catastrophic Incidents

Prior to and during catastrophic incidents, especially those that occur with little or no notice, the Federal Government may mobilize and deploy assets in anticipation of a formal request from the state. Such deployments of significant Federal assets would occur in anticipation of or following catastrophic incidents involving chemical, biological, radiological, nuclear, or high-yield explosive weapons of mass destruction; large-magnitude earthquakes; or other incidents affecting heavily populated areas. Proactive efforts are intended to ensure that Federal resources reach the scene in time to assist in reducing disruption of normal functions of state and local governments and are done in coordination and collaboration with state and local governments, private sector entities, and NGOs when possible.

Federal Response and Assistance Available Without a Stafford Act Declaration

The NRF covers the full range of complex and constantly changing requirements in anticipation of, or in response to, threats or actual incidents. In addition to Stafford Act support, the NRF or other supplementary or complementary operational plans may be applied to respond or provide other forms of support.

Federal Departments and Agencies Acting Under Their Own Authorities

Immediate lifesaving assistance to states, as well as other types of assistance, such as wildland firefighting support or response to an agricultural disease or cybersecurity incident, are performed by Federal departments or agencies under their own authorities and funding or through reciprocal mutual assistance agreements and do not require a Stafford Act declaration. Some Federal departments or agencies conduct or may lead Federal response actions under their own authorities using funding sources other than the President's Disaster Relief Fund. For example, specific trust funds are established under Federal environmental laws to support and fund oil and hazardous substances response operations.

Federal-to-Federal Support

Federal departments and agencies may execute interagency or intra-agency reimbursable agreements in accordance with the Economy Act or other applicable authorities. The Financial Management Support Annex to the NRF contains information about this process. A Federal department or agency responding to an incident under its own authorities may also request support from the Secretary of Homeland Security in obtaining and coordinating additional Federal assistance. The Secretary of Homeland Security may activate one or more ESFs to provide the requested support.

---

[30] Refer to footnote 15 for more information on U.S. possessions and freely associated states.

Coordinating Structures and Integration

Coordinating structures aid preparedness and response at all levels of government and within the private sector, communities, and nongovernmental entities. The structures help organize and measure the whole community's capabilities in order to address the requirements of the Response mission area, facilitate problem solving, improve access to response resources, and foster coordination prior to and following an incident.

Scalable, flexible, and adaptable coordinating structures are essential in aligning the key roles and responsibilities to deliver the Response mission area's core capabilities. The flexibility of such structures helps ensure that communities across the country can organize response efforts to address a variety of risks based on their unique needs, capabilities, demographics, governing structures, and non-traditional partners. The NRF is not based on a one-size-fits-all organizational construct, but instead acknowledges the concept of tiered response, which emphasizes that response to incidents should be handled at the lowest jurisdictional level capable of handling the mission. These structures can be partially or fully implemented in the context of a threat, in anticipation of a significant event, or in response to an incident. Selective implementation allows for a scaled response, delivery of the exact resources that are needed, and a level of coordination appropriate to each incident.

The following section describes the coordinating structures within the Response mission area and explains how they integrate with the coordinating structures that support other mission areas to build preparedness and enhance the Nation's resilience to all types of risks and hazards.

Local Coordinating Structures

Local jurisdictions and states employ a variety of coordinating structures to help identify risks, establish relationships, organize, and build capabilities. Due to the unique partnerships, geographic conditions, threats, and established capabilities each jurisdiction faces, the coordinating structures at these levels vary. Examples of local response coordinating structures include local planning committees, CERTs, and chapters of national-level associations. These structures organize and integrate their capabilities and resources with neighboring jurisdictions, the state, the private sector, and NGOs.

State Coordinating Structures

States also leverage the capabilities and resources of partners across the state when identifying needs and building capabilities. The coordinating structures at the state level also vary depending on factors such as geography, population, industry, and the capabilities of the local jurisdictions within the state. These structures are also designed to leverage appropriate representatives from across the whole community—some of whom may also participate in local or regional coordinating structures. Many states create independent committees or councils focused on specific areas or functions as a sub-set of their emergency management agency. For example, some states have Animal Disaster Planning Advisory Committees that provide important input to statewide response plans on animal issues.

Private Sector Coordinating Structures

Business EOCs, industry trade groups, and private sector information and intelligence centers serve as coordinating structures for the private sector. These organizations, composed of multiple businesses and entities brought together by shared geography or common function (e.g., banking, supply chain management, transportation, venue management), support the collaboration, communication, and sharing of information within the private sector. Such organizations can coordinate with and support NGOs, and in many cases they serve as a conduit to local and state government coordinating structures.

Federal Coordinating Structures

National Security Council

The National Security Council (NSC) is the principal policy body for consideration of national security policy issues requiring Presidential determination. The NSC advises and assists the President in integrating all aspects of national security policy as it affects the United States—domestic, foreign, military, intelligence, and economic (in conjunction with the National Economic Council). Along with its subordinate committees, the NSC is the President's principal means for coordinating Executive Branch departments and agencies in the development and implementation of national security policy.

Emergency Support Functions

The Federal Government and many state governments organize their response resources and capabilities under the ESF construct. ESFs have proven to be an effective way to bundle and manage resources to deliver core capabilities. The Federal ESFs are the primary, but not exclusive, Federal coordinating structures for building, sustaining, and delivering the response core capabilities. The ESFs are vital structures for responding to Stafford Act incidents; however, they may also be used for other incidents. Most Federal ESFs support a number of the response core capabilities. In addition, there are responsibilities and actions associated with Federal ESFs that extend beyond the core capabilities and support other response activities, as well as department and agency responsibilities.

The Federal ESFs bring together the capabilities of Federal departments and agencies and other national-level assets. ESFs are not based on the capabilities of a single department or agency, and the functions for which they are responsible cannot be accomplished by any single department or agency. Instead, Federal ESFs are groups of organizations that work together to deliver core capabilities and support an effective response.

As noted above, many state and local jurisdictions have adopted and tailored the ESF construct. Because state and local jurisdictions establish ESFs based on their specific risks and requirements, there is no mandatory or direct linkage to the Federal ESFs. State and local governments are encouraged to engage members of the whole community as part of whatever coordinating processes they use.

Table 4 summarizes the Federal ESFs and indicates the response core capabilities each ESF most directly supports. All ESFs support the common core capabilities–Planning, Public Information and Warning, and Operational Coordination–and many ESFs support more than those that are listed.

Table 4: Emergency Support Functions and ESF Coordinators

ESF #1—Transportation   **ESF Coordinator: Department of Transportation**
Key Response Core Capability: Critical Transportation
Coordinates the support of management of transportation systems and infrastructure, the regulation of transportation, management of the Nation's airspace, and ensuring the safety and security of the national transportation system. Functions include but are not limited to: ▪ Transportation modes management and control   ▪ Transportation safety   ▪ Stabilization and reestablishment of transportation infrastructure   ▪ Movement restrictions   ▪ Damage and impact assessment.
ESF #2—Communications   **ESF Coordinator: DHS/National Communications System**
Key Response Core Capability: Operational Communications
Coordinates the reestablishment of the critical communications infrastructure, facilitates the stabilization of systems and applications from cyber attacks, and coordinates communications support to response efforts. Functions include but are not limited to: ▪ Coordination with telecommunications and information technology industries   ▪ Reestablishment and repair of telecommunications infrastructure   ▪ Protection, reestablishment, and sustainment of national cyber and information technology resources   ▪ Oversight of communications within the Federal response structures.
ESF #3—Public Works and Engineering   **ESF Coordinator: DOD/U.S. Army Corps of Engineers**
Key Response Core Capabilities: Infrastructure Systems, Critical Transportation, Public and Private Services and Resources, Environmental Response/Health and Safety, Fatality Management, Mass Care Services, Mass Search and Rescue Operations
Coordinates the capabilities and resources to facilitate the delivery of services, technical assistance, engineering expertise, construction management, and other support to prepare for, respond to, and/or recover from a disaster or an incident. Functions include but are not limited to: ▪ Infrastructure protection and emergency repair   ▪ Critical infrastructure reestablishment   ▪ Engineering services and construction management   ▪ Emergency contracting support for lifesaving and life-sustaining services.
ESF #4—Firefighting   **ESF Coordinator: USDA/U.S. Forest Service and DHS/FEMA/U.S. Fire Administration**
Key Response Core Capabilities: Critical Transportation, Operational Communications, Public and Private Services and Resources, Infrastructure Systems, Mass Care Services, Mass Search and Rescue Operations, On-scene Security and Protection, Public Health and Medical Services
Coordinates the support for the detection and suppression of fires. Functions include but are not limited to: ▪ Support to wildland, rural, and urban firefighting operations.

ESF #5—Information and Planning ESF Coordinator: DHS/FEMA
Key Response Core Capabilities: Situational Assessment, Planning, Public Information and Warning
Supports and facilitates multiagency planning and coordination for operations involving incidents requiring Federal coordination. Functions include but are not limited to: ▪ Incident action planning ▪ Information collection, analysis, and dissemination.

ESF #6—Mass Care, Emergency Assistance, Temporary Housing, and Human Services ESF Coordinator: DHS/FEMA
Key Response Core Capabilities: Mass Care Services, Public and Private Services and Resources, Public Health and Medical Services, Critical Transportation, Fatality Management Services
Coordinates the delivery of mass care and emergency assistance, including: ▪ Mass care ▪ Emergency assistance ▪ Disaster housing ▪ Human services.

ESF #7—Logistics ESF Coordinator: General Services Administration and DHS/FEMA
Key Response Core Capabilities: Public and Private Services and Resources, Mass Care Services, Critical Transportation, Infrastructure Systems, Operational Communications
Coordinates comprehensive incident resource planning, management, and sustainment capability to meet the needs of disaster survivors and responders. Functions include but are not limited to: ▪ Comprehensive, national incident logistics planning, management, and sustainment capability ▪ Resource support (e.g., facility space, office equipment and supplies, contracting services).

ESF #8—Public Health and Medical Services ESF Coordinator: Department of Health and Human Services
Key Response Core Capabilities: Public Health and Medical Services, Fatality Management Services, Mass Care Services, Critical Transportation, Public Information and Warning, Environmental Response/Health and Safety, Public and Private Services and Resources
Coordinates the mechanisms for assistance in response to an actual or potential public health and medical disaster or incident. Functions include but are not limited to: ▪ Public health ▪ Medical surge support including patient movement ▪ Behavioral health services ▪ Mass fatality management.

ESF #9—Search and Rescue ESF Coordinator: DHS/FEMA
Key Response Core Capability: Mass Search and Rescue Operations
Coordinates the rapid deployment of search and rescue resources to provide specialized lifesaving assistance. Functions include but are not limited to: ▪ Structural Collapse (Urban) Search and Rescue ▪ Maritime/Coastal/Waterborne Search and Rescue ▪ Land Search and Rescue.

ESF #10—Oil and Hazardous Materials Response
ESF Coordinator: Environmental Protection Agency

Key Response Core Capabilities: Environmental Response/Health and Safety, Critical Transportation, Infrastructure Systems, Public Information and Warning

Coordinates support in response to an actual or potential discharge and/or release of oil or hazardous materials. Functions include but are not limited to:
- Environmental assessment of the nature and extent of oil and hazardous materials contamination
- Environmental decontamination and cleanup.

ESF #11—Agriculture and Natural Resources
ESF Coordinator: Department of Agriculture

Key Response Core Capabilities: Environmental Response/Health and Safety, Mass Care Services, Public Health and Medical Services, Critical Transportation, Public and Private Services and Resources, Infrastructure Systems

Coordinates a variety of functions designed to protect the Nation's food supply, respond to plant and animal pest and disease outbreaks, and protect natural and cultural resources. Functions include but are not limited to:
- Nutrition assistance
- Animal and agricultural health issue response
- Technical expertise, coordination, and support of animal and agricultural emergency management
- Meat, poultry, and processed egg products safety and defense
- Natural and cultural resources and historic properties protection.

ESF #12—Energy
ESF Coordinator: Department of Energy

Key Response Core Capabilities: Infrastructure Systems, Public and Private Services and Resources, Situational Assessment

Facilitates the reestablishment of damaged energy systems and components and provides technical expertise during an incident involving radiological/nuclear materials. Functions include but are not limited to:
- Energy infrastructure assessment, repair, and reestablishment
- Energy industry utilities coordination
- Energy forecast.

ESF #13—Public Safety and Security
ESF Coordinator: Department of Justice/Bureau of Alcohol, Tobacco, Firearms, and Explosives

Key Response Core Capability: On-scene Security and Protection

Coordinates the integration of public safety and security capabilities and resources to support the full range of incident management activities. Functions include but are not limited to:
- Facility and resource security
- Security planning and technical resource assistance
- Public safety and security support
- Support to access, traffic, and crowd control.

ESF #14—Superseded by National Disaster Recovery Framework

ESF #15—External Affairs
ESF Coordinator: DHS

Key Response Core Capability: Public Information and Warning
Coordinates the release of accurate, coordinated, timely, and accessible public information to affected audiences, including the government, media, NGOs, and the private sector. Works closely with state and local officials to ensure outreach to the whole community. Functions include, but are not limited to: ▪ Public affairs and the Joint Information Center ▪ Intergovernmental (local, state, tribal, and territorial) affairs ▪ Congressional affairs ▪ Private sector outreach ▪ Community relations.

ESF Member Roles and Responsibilities

ESFs are not solely attributed to any one organization, nor are they mechanisms for executing an agency's statutory authorities. Each ESF is composed of a department or agency that has been designated as the ESF coordinator along with a number of primary and support agencies. Primary agencies are designated on the basis of their authorities, resources, and capabilities. Support agencies are assigned based on resources or capabilities in a given functional area. To the extent possible, resources provided by the ESFs are identified consistently with NIMS resource typing categories.

- **ESF Coordinators**. ESF coordinators oversee the preparedness activities for a particular ESF and coordinate with its primary and support agencies. Responsibilities of the ESF coordinator include:

  - Maintaining contact with ESF primary and support agencies through conference calls, meetings, training activities, and exercises

  - Monitoring the ESF's progress in meeting the targets of the core capabilities it supports

  - Coordinating efforts with corresponding private sector, NGO, and Federal partners

  - Ensuring the ESF is engaged in appropriate planning and preparedness activities.

- **Primary Agencies.** ESF primary agencies have significant authorities, roles, resources, and capabilities for a particular function within an ESF. Primary agencies are responsible for:

  - Orchestrating support within their functional area for the appropriate response core capabilities and other ESF missions

  - Notifying and requesting assistance from support agencies

  - Managing mission assignments (in Stafford Act incidents) and coordinating with support agencies, as well as appropriate state officials, operations centers, and other stakeholders

  - Coordinating resources resulting from mission assignments

  - Working with all types of organizations to maximize the use of all available resources

  - Monitoring progress in achieving core capability targets and other ESF missions, and providing that information as part of situational and periodic readiness or preparedness assessments

- Planning for incident management, short-term recovery operations, and the transition to long-term recovery

- Maintaining trained personnel to support interagency emergency response and support teams

- Identifying new equipment or capabilities required to prevent or respond to new or emerging threats and hazards or to validate and improve capabilities to address changing risks

- Promoting physical accessibility, programmatic inclusion, and effective communication for the whole community, including individuals with disabilities.

- **Support Agencies.** ESF support agencies have specific capabilities or resources that support primary agencies in executing the mission of the ESF. The activities of support agencies typically include:

  - Participating in planning for incident management, short-term recovery operations, transition to long-term-recovery, and the development of supporting operational plans, standard operating procedures (SOPs), checklists, or other job aids

  - Providing input to periodic readiness assessments

  - Maintaining trained personnel to support interagency emergency response and support teams

  - Identifying new equipment or capabilities required to respond to new or emerging threats and hazards, or to improve the ability to address existing threats

  - Coordinating resources resulting from response mission assignments.

- **Emergency Support Function Leaders Group (ESFLG).** The ESFLG comprises the Federal departments and agencies that are designated as coordinators for ESFs or coordinating agencies for other NRF annexes. FEMA leads the ESFLG and is responsible for calling meetings and other administrative functions. The ESFLG provides a forum for departments and agencies with roles in Federal incident response to jointly address topics such as policies, preparedness, and training.

ESF Activation

Departments and agencies supporting Federal ESFs may be selectively activated by FEMA or as directed by the Secretary of Homeland Security to support response activities for both Stafford Act and non-Stafford Act incidents. Not all incidents requiring Federal support result in the activation of ESFs.

When departments and agencies supporting Federal ESFs are activated, they may assign staff at headquarters, regional, and incident levels. Through the Stafford Act and in accordance with 6 U.S. Code 741 (4) and 753 (c), FEMA may issue mission assignments at all levels to obtain resources and services from Federal departments and agencies across the ESFs.

ESFs are the primary, but not exclusive, response coordinating structures at the Federal level for Stafford Act incidents. Communities, states, regions, and other Federal departments and agencies may use the ESF construct, or they may employ other coordinating structures or partners appropriate to their location, threats, or authorities. Whatever structures are used, they are encouraged to work closely with Federal ESFs at the incident, regional, or headquarters levels if they are activated.

One example of a unique Federal coordinating structure is described below:

- **Tribal Assistance Coordination Group (TAC-G).** Governments at the Federal, state, and local levels foster effective government-to-government working relationships with tribes to achieve the common goal of responding to disasters impacting tribal lands. The TAC-G comprises multiple Federal organizations that are dedicated to cooperation and collaboration to strengthen emergency management as it relates to the over 560 federally-recognized tribal nations.

Non-Stafford Act Coordinating Structures

Although the Federal ESFs are designed to coordinate Federal response resources for both Stafford Act and non-Stafford Act incidents, the ESFs may not always be the most appropriate response coordinating structures for non-Stafford Act incidents. For incidents in which there is no Stafford declaration, the department or agency with primary legal authority may activate the coordinating structures appropriate to that authority. These structures are generally organized consistently with NIMS concepts and principles. In addition to their own structures, departments or agencies responding under their own legal authorities may request the Secretary of Homeland Security to activate relevant ESFs. Pursuant to Presidential directive, the Secretary of Homeland Security coordinates with the head of the department or agency with primary legal authority but retains the authority to activate ESFs or other coordinating structures, as appropriate.

NRF Support Annexes

The NRF Support Annexes describe other mechanisms by which support is organized among private sector, NGO, and Federal partners. Federal departments and agencies designated as coordinating and cooperating agencies in NRF support annexes conduct a variety of activities to include managing specific functions and missions and providing Federal support within their functional areas. The Support Annexes include:

- Critical Infrastructure

- Financial Management

- International Coordination

- Private Sector Coordination

- Tribal Coordination

- Volunteer and Donations Management

- Worker Safety and Health.

NRF Incident Annexes

NRF Incident Annexes describe coordinating structures, in addition to the ESFs, that may be used to deliver core capabilities and support response missions that are unique to a specific type of incident. Incident annexes also describe specialized response teams and resources, incident-specific roles and responsibilities, and other scenario-specific considerations. NRF Incident Annexes address the following contingencies or hazards:

- Biological Incident

- Catastrophic Incident

- Cyber Incident

- Food and Agriculture Incident

- Mass Evacuation Incident

- Nuclear/Radiological Incident

- Terrorism Incident Law Enforcement and Investigation.

Operations Coordination

Response operations involve multiple partners and stakeholders. Operations coordination occurs at all government levels and consists of actions and activities that enable decision makers to determine appropriate courses of action and provide oversight for complex homeland security operations to achieve unity of effort and effective outcomes.

Local Response Operational Structures

Emergency responders at all levels of government use ICS command and coordinating structures to manage response operations (see Figure 2). ICS is a management system designed to integrate facilities, equipment, personnel, procedures, and communications within a common organizational structure.

At the local level, coordinating structures are usually composed of entities within a specific functional area such as public works, law enforcement, emergency medical services, and fire departments. Integration among these structures occurs at an ICP, which provides on-scene incident command and management.

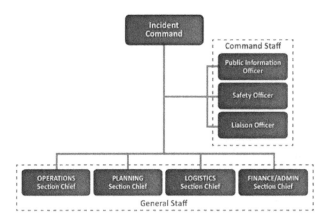

Figure 2: Incident Command Structure

ICS is widely used by all levels of government, as well as by private sector organizations and NGOs to organize field-level operations for a broad spectrum of incidents. Typically, the incident response is structured to facilitate activities in five areas: command, operations, planning, logistics, and finance/administration.

Emergency personnel may also use the Multiagency Coordination System (MACS). The primary function of MACS, as defined in NIMS, is to coordinate activities above the incident level and to prioritize competing demands for incident resources. MACS consist of personnel, procedures, protocols, facilities, business practices, and communications integrated into a common system. MACS elements at the local level include EOCs and coordination centers.

If the local incident commander determines that additional resources or capabilities are needed, he or she contacts the local EOC and relays requirements to the local emergency manager. Local EOCs are the physical locations where multiagency coordination typically occurs and where a variety of local coordinating structures come together to solve problems. EOCs help form a common operating picture of the incident, relieve on-scene command of the burden of external coordination, and secure additional resources to help meet response requirements.

EOCs at all levels of government may also encourage participation by the private sector, NGOs, academia, associations, racial and ethnic organizations, and access and functional needs subject matter experts. These members of the whole community, in turn, often maintain their own structures, such as nongovernmental or private sector EOCs.

State Response Operational Structures

The local incident command structure directs on-scene incident management activities and maintains command and control of on-scene incident operations. State EOCs are activated as necessary to support local EOCs and to ensure that responders have the resources they need to conduct response activities. This is achieved through integration of state-level coordinating structures working with local coordinating structures or the local incident command structure.

State Emergency Operations Center

State EOCs are the physical location where multiagency coordination occurs through state-level coordinating structures. Every state maintains an EOC to manage incidents requiring state-level assistance (see Figure 3). Some states have additional EOCs for coordinating information and resources within a region or area.

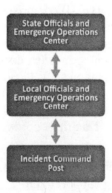

Figure 3: State and Local Response Structure

State EOCs are typically organized by a combination of ESFs or other coordinating structures aligned to disciplines or capabilities. Many states involve their tribal counterparts within the EOC to ensure that tribal coordinating structures are integrated into the delivery of capabilities and that tribal needs are addressed.

Federal Response Operational Structures

When an incident occurs that exceeds, or is anticipated to exceed, local or state resources—or when an incident is managed by Federal departments or agencies acting under their own authorities—the Federal Government may use the management structures described within the NRF. Additionally, the Federal Government may use supplementary or complementary plans to involve all necessary department and agency resources to organize the Federal response and ensure coordination among all response partners.

All Federal departments and agencies may play significant roles in response activities depending on the nature and size of an incident. Many of the arrangements by which departments and agencies participate are defined in the ESF Annexes, coordinated through pre-scripted mission assignments in a Stafford Act response, formalized in interagency agreements, or described in NRF supplementary plans.

The following sections describe Federal support operations at the incident, regional, and headquarters levels.

Federal Incident-level Operations

To help deliver Federal support or response at the incident level, coordinating structures are aligned to incident-level structures. The following section describes the Federal coordinating structures typically associated with Stafford Act incidents. These structures may also be used for Federal-to-Federal support or other non-Stafford Act threats or incidents such as an NSSE.

Unified Coordination

Unified Coordination is the term used to describe the primary state/Federal incident management activities conducted at the incident level. Unified Coordination is typically directed from a Joint Field Office (JFO), a temporary Federal facility that provides a central location for coordination of response efforts by the private sector, NGOs, and all levels of government. Unified Coordination is organized, staffed, and managed in a manner consistent with NIMS principles using the NIMS/ICS structure. The Unified Coordination Group (UCG) comprises senior leaders representing Federal and state interests and, in certain circumstances, tribal governments, local jurisdictions, and the private sector. UCG members must have significant jurisdictional responsibility and authority. The composition of the UCG varies from incident to incident depending on the scope and nature of the disaster. The UCG leads the unified coordination staff. Personnel from state and Federal departments and agencies, other jurisdictional entities, the private sector, and NGOs may be assigned to the unified coordination staff at various incident facilities (e.g., JFO, staging areas, and other field offices). The UCG determines staffing of the unified coordination staff based on incident requirements.

Although Unified Coordination is based on the ICS structure, it does not manage on-scene operations. Instead, it focuses on providing support to on-scene response efforts and conducting broader support operations that may extend beyond the incident site. Unified Coordination must include robust operations, planning, public information, and logistics capabilities that integrate local, state, and Federal—as well as tribal, territorial, and insular area governments—personnel when appropriate, so that all levels of government work together to achieve unity of effort.

When incidents affect multiple localities and states or the entire Nation, multiple UCGs with associated unified coordination staff may be established. In these situations, coordination occurs according to the principles of area command as described in NIMS.

As the primary field entity for Federal response, Unified Coordination integrates diverse Federal authorities and capabilities and coordinates Federal response and recovery operations. Figure 4 depicts a Unified Coordination organization that might be assembled to deal with a major incident, such as a terrorist attack, that includes a law enforcement dimension. Federal agencies that conduct on-scene, tactical level activities under the Stafford Act may also establish incident and area command structures, generally in conjunction with their counterpart local, state, tribal, and/or insular area agencies, to manage that work.

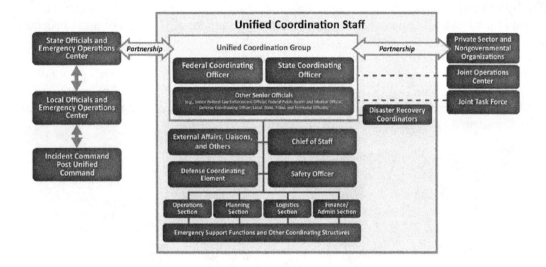

Figure 4: Unified Coordination

Federal Incident-level Operations for Non-Stafford Act Incidents

For non-Stafford Act incidents, the department or agency with primary legal jurisdiction activates the response structures appropriate to its authorities; these structures are generally organized based on NIMS concepts and principles. When coordinating pursuant to Presidential directive, the Secretary of Homeland Security coordinates with the head of the department or agency with primary legal jurisdiction but retains the authority to activate the additional response structures the Secretary determines appropriate.

Federal Incident Command/Area Command in Non-Stafford Act Incidents

In non-Stafford Act incidents, Federal agencies who have responsibility for on-scene, tactical-level operations may establish incident command and area command structures, or coordinate with state and local agencies to form unified incident command and unified area command structures.

Federal Regional Operational Support

Coordinating structures can be assembled and organized at the regional level to address incidents that cross state borders or have broad geographic or system-wide implications or to manage competing requirements for response assets among multiple incidents.

Federal Regional Facilities

Most Federal departments and agencies have regional or field offices that may participate with state and local governments in planning for incidents and provide response assets when an incident occurs in their jurisdiction. Some Federal departments and agencies share the same standard Federal regional structure as FEMA. In larger-scale incidents, these regional and field offices may provide the initial response assets with additional support being provided from other department and agency offices across the Nation. Some Federal regional and field offices have their own EOCs to support deployments of their assets.

- **FEMA Regional Response Coordination Center (RRCC).** FEMA has 10 regional offices, each headed by a Regional Administrator (see Figure 5). Each of FEMA's regional offices maintains an RRCC. When activated, RRCCs are multi-agency coordination centers generally staffed by ESFs in anticipation of or immediately following an incident. Operating under the direction of the FEMA Regional Administrator, the staff within the RRCCs coordinates Federal regional response efforts and maintains connectivity with FEMA Headquarters and with state EOCs, state and major urban area fusion centers, Federal Executive Boards, and other Federal and state operations and coordination centers that potentially contribute to the development of situational awareness. The UCG assumes responsibility for coordinating Federal response activities at the incident level once Unified Coordination is established, freeing the RRCC to deal with new incidents should they occur.

Figure 5: FEMA Regions

Federal Headquarters Operational Support

Coordinating structures are assembled and organized at the headquarters level, particularly to address incidents that cross regional borders or have broad geographic or system-wide implications.

Federal Operations Centers

Most Cabinet-level departments and agencies have at least one headquarters-level operations center. A wide range of such centers maintain situational awareness within their functional areas and provide relevant information to the National Operations Center (NOC). These operations centers may also coordinate ESF activities, communicate with other Federal operations centers, and communicate with their local, state, tribal, territorial, and insular area government counterparts. Examples of Federal Operations Centers include:

- **National Operations Center (NOC).** In the event of an act of terrorism, natural disaster, or other emergency, the National Operations Center (NOC),[31] as the principal operations center for the Department of Homeland Security, coordinates and integrates information from NOC components to provide situational awareness and a common operating picture for the entire

---

[31] The NOC is more than a brick and mortar command center. It is composed of the NOC Watch, Intelligence Watch and Warning, FEMA National Watch Center and National Response Coordination Center, and the National Infrastructure Coordinating Center. The DHS National Cybersecurity and Communications Integration Center also maintains and updates the NOC regarding the national common operational picture for cyberspace.

Federal Government, as well as for local, tribal, and state governments, as appropriate, to ensure that accurate and critical terrorism and disaster-related information reaches government decision makers in a timely manner. Additionally, the NOC serves as the national fusion center, collecting and synthesizing all-source information, including information from state and major urban area fusion centers, for all threats and hazards across the entire integrated national preparedness system.

- **National Response Coordination Center (NRCC).** When activated, the NRCC is a multiagency coordination center located at FEMA Headquarters. Its staff coordinates the overall Federal support for major disasters and emergencies, including catastrophic incidents and emergency management program implementation. FEMA maintains the NRCC as a functional component of the NOC for incident support operations.

- **National Military Command Center (NMCC).** DOD's NMCC is the Nation's focal point for continuous monitoring and coordination of worldwide military operations. It directly supports combatant commanders, the Chairman of the Joint Chiefs of Staff, the Secretary of Defense, and the President in the command of U.S. Armed Forces in peacetime contingencies and war. The NMCC participates in a wide variety of activities, ranging from missile warning and attack assessment to management of peacetime operations such as Defense Support of Civil Authorities during national emergencies.

- **Strategic Information and Operations Center (SIOC).** The SIOC acts as the FBI's worldwide EOC. The SIOC maintains situational awareness of criminal or terrorist threats, critical incidents and crises, both foreign and domestic, regardless of cause or origin, and provides FBI headquarters executives, domestic field offices, and overseas legal attachés with timely notification and the dissemination of strategic information. The SIOC shares information and intelligence with other EOCs at all levels of government. Maintaining a constant state of readiness to support any crisis or major event, the SIOC provides a secure venue to support crisis management, special event monitoring, and significant operations. It provides command, control, communications connectivity, and a common operating picture for managing FBI operational responses and assets anywhere in the world on behalf of FBI Headquarters divisions, field offices, and legal attachés. In the event of a crisis, the SIOC establishes the headquarters command post and develops connectivity to field command posts and Joint Operations Centers.

The specific structures that are activated for any given incident depend on the levels of government involved, as well as the legal authorities under which the response is being conducted.

Integration

Effective emergency response requires the ability for the response coordinating structures to link to and share information with the coordinating structures in the other mission areas. For example, in the wake of a terrorist attack that results in the need for a coordinated Federal response, Response mission area coordinating structures must work closely with those in the Prevention, Protection, Mitigation, and Recovery mission areas. Effective mitigation efforts directly reduce the required scale of response operations. Prevention and protection activities continue after an attack to prevent and protect from follow-on attacks. This requires close coordination of prevention and protection activities with response and recovery efforts. Integration of response mission activities with protection efforts may also occur in the context of a credible threat. Following determination of such a threat, Protection mission area organizations may switch to an enhanced steady-state posture. At that time, Response mission area assets may need to be positioned to respond quickly should protection, mitigation, and prevention efforts fail. Establishing close working relationships, lines of communication, and coordination protocols between protection, prevention, response, and recovery organizations facilitates this process.

Examples of Response mission area coordinating structures cooperating with other mission area assets include:

- Coordinating with Prevention and Protection mission area structures to share threat information including issuing watches, warnings, and other emergency bulletins

- Coordinating with Protection mission area structures in the wake of an incident to ensure that communities and emergency responders have the protection needed to perform their jobs

- Coordinating anticipatory Response mission area activities with the Mitigation and Recovery mission activities.

Although they are generally considered to be prevention or protection focused organizations, the various state and major urban area fusion centers are examples of coordinating structures whose utility spans mission areas. The collection, analysis, and dissemination of information by the fusion centers can inform response activities through information sharing and operational coordination efforts.

Because of the natural relationship between response and recovery efforts and the fact that response and recovery activities often occur simultaneously, the responsibilities of some ESFs overlap with or transition to the responsibilities of Recovery Support Functions (RSFs), the Recovery mission area coordinating structures defined in the National Disaster Recovery Framework. The RSFs frequently build on the ESF resources and short-term recovery efforts applied by the ESFs to meet basic human needs to integrate short-term recovery efforts with intermediate and long-term recovery needs. The relationships and integration between the ESFs and the coordinating structures of other mission areas are detailed in the FIOPs.

Relationship to Other Mission Areas

All five mission areas integrate with each other through interdependencies, shared assets, and overlapping objectives. These overlapping areas are identified through comprehensive planning with the whole community to ensure that they are addressed during response to an incident.

The Response mission area integrates with the other four mission areas in the following manner:

- **Prevention.** Response organizations coordinate with those responsible for preventing imminent acts of terrorism to understand potential and specific threats and to prepare accordingly by planning for general threats and through crisis action planning for credible threats. Response mission area capabilities must be available in case efforts to prevent terrorist attacks fail or credible threats are identified. Coordinating with prevention officials aids response officials in understanding the extraordinary response capabilities that terrorist attacks may require. When response activities are occurring, whether due to a terrorist attack or another type of incident, prevention activities continue.

- **Protection.** Efforts to protect people and communities, as well as vital facilities, systems, and resources, are inextricably linked to response efforts. Responders that support the Protection and Recovery mission areas include many of the same people and organizations. Protection activities occur before, during, and after incidents. In the aftermath of an incident, a physically secure environment should be established before Response mission area organizations can deliver essential response capabilities.

- **Mitigation.** Reducing risk through hazard mitigation reduces requirements for response capabilities. Mitigation organizations often have special insight into risks and hazards that can be shared with response personnel to improve response planning and execution.

- **Recovery.** As with Protection, the Response and Recovery mission areas include some of the same people and organizations. Communities should build general recovery plans before an incident occurs. After an incident, recovery efforts must begin as soon as possible, often while response capabilities are still being applied.

Operational Planning

Planning across the full range of homeland security operations is an inherent responsibility of every level of government. This NRF fosters unity of effort for emergency operations planning by providing common doctrine and purpose.

A plan is a continuous, evolving instrument of anticipated actions that maximizes opportunities and guides response operations. Since planning is an ongoing process, a plan is a product based on information and understanding at the moment and is subject to revision.

Operational planning is conducted across the whole community, including the private sector, NGOs, and all levels of government. Comprehensive Preparedness Guide (CPG) 101 provides further information on the various types of plans and guidance on the fundamentals of planning.

From the Federal perspective, integrated planning helps explain how Federal departments and agencies and other national-level whole community partners provide the right resources at the right time to support local, state, tribal, territorial, and insular area government response operations. From their perspectives, integrated planning provides answers to questions about which traditional and non-traditional partners can provide the necessary resources.

The following section outlines how operational planning is applied within the Response mission area and provides guidance for the development of the Response FIOP.

Response Operational Planning

Federal Planning

At the Federal level, the NRF is supported by the Response FIOP. The concepts in the NRF and NIMS guide Federal operational response planning and development of the Response FIOP, which provides further information regarding roles and responsibilities, identifies the critical tasks an entity will take in executing core capabilities, and identifies resourcing and sourcing requirements.

The Response FIOP further defines the concepts, principles, structures, and actions introduced in this Framework with a specific focus on these elements at the Federal level. It addresses interdependencies and integration with the other mission areas throughout the plan's concept of operations. It also describes the management of concurrent actions and coordination points with the areas of prevention, protection, mitigation, and recovery.

The Response FIOP takes an all-hazards approach to preparedness, highlights key areas of interoperability across the five mission areas, and addresses the whole community to optimize resources. The concept of operations in the Response FIOP is based on a no-notice catastrophic incident that spans multiple regions and states and assumes hundreds of thousands of casualties, severe damage to critical infrastructure, and limited ingress and egress due to massive damage to transportation systems. Such an incident would have significant ramifications on the political, economic, social, environmental, logistical, technical, legal, and administrative structures and would overwhelm local, state, tribal, territorial, and insular area government response capabilities.

While the planning factors used for the Response FIOP suggest an incident that will result in a Stafford Act declaration, the plan also addresses the responsibility of certain Federal departments and agencies to lead elements of a response under their own authorities.

The Response FIOP contains:

- A detailed concept of operations
- A description of critical tasks and responsibilities
- Detailed resourcing, personnel, and sourcing requirements
- Specific provisions for the rapid integration of resources and personnel to incidents caused by any of the hazards/threats to which the whole community is particularly vulnerable
- Functional and incident-specific annexes as necessary.

It does not contain detailed descriptions of specific department or agency functions as such information is located in department- or agency-level operational plans.

The NRF is based on the concept of tiered response with an understanding that most incidents start at the local level, and as needs exceed resources and capabilities, additional local, state, and Federal assets are applied. The Response FIOP, therefore, is intended to align with other local, state, tribal, territorial, insular area government, and Federal plans to ensure that all response partners share a common operational focus. Similarly, integration occurs at the Federal level among the departments, agencies, and nongovernmental partners that compose the respective mission area through the frameworks, FIOPs, and departmental and agency operations plans.

In developing the Response FIOP, the following planning needs are taken into account:

- Food and water
- Physically accessible evacuation and sheltering
- Accessible transportation
- Medical surge, medical countermeasures, and treatment capability
- General and medical supplies, durable medical equipment, and disability-related assistance/FNSS
- Emotional, behavioral, and mental health needs
- Reunification and safety of unaccompanied minors
- Guardianship
- Accessible communications
- Animal emergency management needs.

Planning Assumptions

The detailed planning factors for the Response FIOP focus on the impacts associated with a large-scale emergency or disaster that could occur anywhere within the continental United States, its territories, or insular area governments and results in a substantial number of fatalities and injuries, widespread property loss, and disruption of essential services across a large geographic area. Such an occurrence has significant ramifications on the political, economic, social, environmental, logistical, technical, legal, and administrative structures within the impacted area and may overwhelm governmental response capabilities.

The plan addresses the potential, unique requirements and needs of all members of the whole community. While the Response FIOP contains assumptions for each of the response core capabilities, some of the overarching assumptions include the following:

- Multiple catastrophic incidents or attacks will occur with little or no warning

- Incidents are typically managed at the lowest possible geographic, organizational, and jurisdictional level

- Incident management activities will be initiated and conducted using the principles contained in NIMS

- The combined expertise and capabilities of government at all levels, the private sector, and NGOs will be required to respond to a catastrophic incident.

Framework Application

Implementation of the concepts within the NRF and Response FIOP is mandatory for Federal departments and agencies. While the NRF does not direct the actions of other response elements, the guidance contained in the NRF and the Response FIOP is intended to inform local, state, tribal, territorial, and insular area governments, as well as NGOs and the private sector, regarding how the Federal Government responds to incidents. These partners can use this information to inform their planning and ensure that assumptions regarding Federal assistance and response and the manner in which Federal support will be provided are accurate.

Supporting Resources

To assist NRF users, FEMA will maintain an online repository that contains electronic versions of the current NRF documents—base document, ESF Annexes, Support Annexes, and Incident Annexes—as well as other supporting materials. This Resource Center will provide information, training materials, and other tools, such as an overview of the main Stafford Act provisions, a guide to authorities and references, and an abbreviation list to assist response partners in understanding and executing their roles under the NRF.

Resource Center materials will be regularly evaluated, updated, and augmented as necessary. Additional content may be added or modified at the request of Response mission area partners and other users.

Conclusion

The environment in which the Nation operates grows ever more complex and unpredictable. In implementing the NRF to build national preparedness, partners are encouraged to develop a shared understanding of broad-level strategic implications as they make critical decisions in building future capacity and capability. The whole community should be engaged in examining and implementing the strategy and doctrine contained in this Framework, considering both current and future requirements in the process. This means that this Framework is a living document, and it will be regularly reviewed to evaluate consistency with existing and new policies, evolving conditions, and the experience gained from its use. The first review will be completed no later than 18 months after the release of the Framework. Subsequent reviews will be conducted in order to evaluate the effectiveness of the Framework on a quadrennial basis.

DHS will coordinate and oversee the review and maintenance process for the NRF. The revision process includes developing or updating any documents necessary to carry out capabilities. Significant updates to the Framework will be vetted through a Federal senior-level interagency review process. This Framework will be reviewed in order to accomplish the following:

- Assess and update information on the core capabilities in support of Response goals and objectives

- Ensure that it adequately reflects the organization of responsible entities

- Ensure that it is consistent with the other four mission areas

- Update processes based on changes in the national threat/hazard environment

- Incorporate lessons learned and effective practices from day-to-day operations, exercises, and actual incidents and alerts

- Reflect progress in the Nation's Response mission activities, the need to execute new laws, executive orders, and Presidential directives, as well as strategic changes to national priorities and guidance, critical tasks, or national capabilities.

The implementation and review of this Framework will consider effective practices and lessons learned from exercises and operations, as well as pertinent new processes and technologies. Effective practices include continuity planning, which ensures that the capabilities contained in this Framework can continue to be executed regardless of the threat or hazard. Pertinent new processes and technologies should enable the Nation to adapt efficiently to the evolving risk environment and use data relating to location, context, and interdependencies that allow for effective integration across all missions using a standards-based approach. Updates to the NRF Annexes may occur independently from reviews of the base document.

America's security and resilience work is never finished. While the Nation is safer, stronger, and better prepared than it was a decade ago, the commitment to safeguard the Nation against its greatest risks, now and for decades to come, remains resolute. By bringing the whole community together now to address future needs, the Nation will continue to improve its preparedness to face whatever challenges unfold.

CPSIA information can be obtained
at www.ICGtesting.com
Printed in the USA
LVHW102314141218
600581LV00005B/17/P